Millions of years ago, as the ancient split apart, the tectonic plates which make up the earth's crust drifted precariously on a sea of molten rock, jostling, fighting and releasing material of unimaginable temperatures into the world above. As time passed by, a vast expanse of ocean, the Pacific, became encircled by massive volcanoes and deep trenches now known as the Ring of Fire.

The 17,000 islands of Indonesia emerged, as the Eurasian, Philippine, Australian and Pacific plates battled for space and created one of the most volcanically active regions of the world. Within it is the placid Lake Toba in Sumatra, 100 kilometres in length and formed 70,000 years ago by an eruption which covered the distant country of India in ash as much as 6 metres deep.

Then there is Mount Tambora in Sumbawa, whose eruption in 1815 cancelled summer in Europe and America the following year. And, of course, there is Krakatoa, just west of the island of Java, which in 1883 blew itself apart in an explosion heard almost 5,000 kilometres away.

Close to the remains of these events, 8 degrees south of the equator, lie Bali and Lombok, two beautiful islands split by a narrow stretch of sea but which were far enough apart in ancient times that they helped our understanding of evolution and brought us closer to answering the great questions of life. One of them is regarded as an island paradise, the other contains one of the highest volcanoes in south-east Asia.

The politics of the area are as turbulent as the environment – fertile lands at the mercy of storms, earthquakes, explosions and unrest. The people are a complex mix of many ancient tribes, cultures and religions – they are proud of their heritage and work hard to make a living.

On the other side of the world is a medium-sized island with its own complex mix of ancient tribes. In a small house a table shakes and a cup of tea leaves a beige ring on an economics textbook. The television is showing a fat purple creature dancing with a handbag.

Next to a newspaper is a scrappy bit of paper with one word – 'Rinjani'.

Playing with Fire

Nick Langston-Able

Best wishes.

Nick

freak ash
BOOKS

Published in the United Kingdom in 2007 by Freak Ash Books, a trade name of Freak Ash Ltd.

www.freakash.net

Cover design by Simon Burn.

Photographs reproduced with the permission of the author.

A CIP catalogue record for this book is available from the British library.

ISBN 978 0 9553403 4 5

Printed and bound by Trade Print Europe Ltd, London.
72 New Bond Street, London, W1S 1RR

For anyone who takes the road less travelled by.

Apologies and Acknowledgements

Publishing a book is both exciting and daunting so my first acknowledgement goes to you, the reader, for getting this far; I am grateful to you for picking it up and I hope you enjoy the rest.

The book is a true account of my journey through Indonesia and is based on the relatively comprehensive diary notes I took at the time and memories sparked by photographs. The conversations are virtually word-for-word. I have tried to keep it that way in order to keep it authentic – I hope you feel that you are there.

This, however, leads to some pre-emptive apologies. Firstly, I apologise to the wonderful and less wonderful people I met if any description of them is not quite how they remember themselves – I'm as confident as I can be in my recollections. Secondly, I apologise to the people of Indonesia if my spellings or translations of any words are inept or wrong – I assure you I did my best. Thirdly, I apologise for having real problems finding out certain distances and altitudes – on Lombok, for example, this did not seem to be an exact science, so I have done the best I can with the available evidence. Fourthly, I apologise for the over-use of the word 'caldera' – it is the correct technical term for the collapse of a volcano's magma (molten rock) chamber once a large amount of the lava has emptied out during an eruption; therefore it tends to be a particularly large kind of crater, often many kilometres across, and you wouldn't want to be around when it happened.

Which leads to my first acknowledgement, which is to Pliny who wrote about the famous eruption of Mount Vesuvius and who captured my imagination when I read about it at school. Secondly, to the backpackers I have met on my travels who have helped make every experience so memorable and particularly my travelling companions in Indonesia. Thirdly, to friends and family who have supported me and shown an interest – you have heard the stories, looked at the photos, read the rough drafts and had trouble comprehending my wish to be over-adventurous in far-off places; this book is the best way I have of explaining it. Fourthly, a particular mention to my grandparents who told stories to a boy who had never travelled about life in Penang and developed my fascination for South-East Asia; I'm glad Grandad was able to read this – sorry about the swearing. Fifthly, to Michael Sanders and the team at Freak Ash who turned this project into a true partnership and to whom I will always be grateful.

And finally, to Indonesia itself, an extraordinary country full of people who have, most of the time, treated me with great hospitality and whom I admire and respect. It is a country that I love.

Terima kasih.

Playing with Fire

Tired

Life is like a mountain –
the view from the top is wonderful
but getting there requires great struggle

The narrow ridge leading up to the summit stretched towards Orion who was lying on his side ahead of me, fantastically bright and a clear guide. As I gained in altitude and the direction of the rim curved in a more southerly direction, the wind became increasingly fierce, striking the unprotected east side of the rim and gusting over the top. The force was relentless and I wondered how hard it would have to be to send me flying into the crater lake, 1500 metres below me. My legs were now screaming. Every time I tried to gain a foothold I slipped back and felt huge amounts of energy draining away. The ridge was ever steeper now and even areas of harder rock were giving away beneath my feet; scrambling for handholds was pointless. I was taking three or four steps and then stopping each time, perhaps gaining a metre. At this point the only thing I could do was yell at myself, something I would normally have thought was ridiculous but at that moment seemed the only constructive thing I could manage.

Four weeks earlier I'd been bored. I was thirty (going on twenty-one), with friends acquiring kids and a house that needed decorating. That's when it happened. I was hit on the side of the head; by a cliché – life's too short. I decided to do something about it.

Vague Plans

Lecturer, 30, single, tall, handsome, solvent, likes music and travel,
WLTM slightly mad vegetarian female
with large hands and an interest in animals

Responses to boredom can be varied. Caged primates, for example, have been witnessed exhibiting behaviour such as listlessness, excessive masturbation, unprovoked aggression, and watching too much daytime television. I should have been at work. It was a Monday morning and I was contemplating life through the medium of Tinky-Winky, Dipsy, La-La and Po who were attempting to communicate with a mischievous vacuum cleaner whilst singing a song about toast.

Flicking through Saturday's papers, I spotted the flight to Jakarta just as the creepy sun was setting over Teletubbyland. I had read about Indonesia as a travel destination and this had coincided with a childhood wish mysteriously rearing its head – I wanted to see a volcano. Indonesia was apparently one of the most volcanically active places in the world. What's more it seemed that many of the volcanoes could be climbed and one, Rinjani, rose from the sea to nearly as high as the Matterhorn and the Eiger. I had backpacked around south-east Asia before and had desperately wanted to return. Indonesia seemed like the ultimate destination with its incredible mix of ancient temples, massive volcanoes, rainforest and beaches. The killer blow was the BBC.

"The death toll in Indonesia has reached more than two hundred after the last four days of riots, looting and protests . . . charred corpses of more than one hundred people . . . killed when a shopping mall was set on fire in the capital city, Jakarta . . . worst period of civil unrest to hit the country in more than thirty years . . . violence has been triggered by economic and political unrest . . . what began as student demonstrations has now descended into mass protests and rioting . . . foreigners are leaving the country . . . tanks and armoured vehicles are patrolling the streets . . . utter and total anarchy . . . people running riot and looters wandering freely around Jakarta."

Quite how and why this encouraged me is unclear. It wasn't that I had a morbid fascination in scenes of carnage; it was the allure of witnessing first-hand the effects of such massive changes added to the arrogance of someone who felt he could wander around a country in economic turmoil and remain completely unaffected by it. As everyone else was sheltering from the thunderstorm I'd be climbing a tree wearing a metal hat.

I picked up the tickets on Tuesday morning – Lufthansa to Jakarta. I had acquired a couple of books on the areas in which I was interested – Java, Bali, Lombok – and began to wonder how on earth I was going to do all the things I wanted in four weeks. I scrounged advice from a couple of friends, did some research and came up with a vague plan. A thousand mile trip across three islands taking in temples, volcanoes and anything else Indonesia had to offer.

I didn't mind vague. A good journey creates itself; it develops its own personality and takes you where it wishes. The element of not knowing who's controlling whom is part of the whole point of travel (though admittedly this can be quite frustrating when you're trying to get home for *Neighbours*[1]).

---

1 The popular issue-based TV drama series set in Australia and watched by educated people following a hard day's work.

What did I know about volcanoes?

1 – When I was very young I had a book entitled *The Earth*.

2 – When I was eleven I read a book called *Volcano Adventure* by Willard Price featuring two characters that I think were called Hal and Roger who had lots of adventures.

3 – When I was fifteen I learnt about Pompeii and Vesuvius and have never forgotten AD79 as an important historical date.

4 – That's it.

5 – Might need to do some research.

Reactions to my trip were supportive.

"You're going where?"

"Indonesia."

"Oh. Where's that?"

The more knowledgeable offered help.

"Aren't they rioting there?"

Some were keen vulcanologists.

"Volcanoes? Aren't they dangerous?"

And others were medical experts.

"I've heard you need loads of injections. I don't like needles."

Luckily I had enough tetanus, typhoid, hepatitis and other hard-to-spell words in my bloodstream not to have to worry about further auditions as a pin-cushion. I had also heard a rumour from at least two people that if you took vitamin B tablets you wouldn't get malaria – that makes it a medical fact.

I was, however, able to impress with amazing pub trivia.

Pub trivia 1

Indonesia claimed independence from the Dutch in 1945. (Not very interesting really.)

Pub trivia 2

Indonesia has a population of over 200,000,000, making it the fourth most populous country in the world after China, India and USA. The UK has 60,000,000. (Quite interesting.)

Pub trivia 3

Indonesia has an area of around 1,900,000KM ("Slightly less than three times the size of Texas", according to the CIA World Factbook) compared to the UK's 244,000KM. ("Slightly smaller than Oregon", apparently.)

Pub trivia 4

Indonesia's 1997 inflation rate was 77%, compared to a UK inflation rate of 3% (Of interest to economists.)

Pub trivia 5

According to my 1975 world atlas and a plastic ruler it is nearly 6,000 kilometres (4,000 miles) end to end, further than London to New York. (Amazing.)

My packing skills had been refined by previous trips. A backpack should be able to: a) sit on your lap on a bus; b) fit through the window of a Jeep; c) be light enough to carry for at least 40 minutes in equatorial heat. I decided to take the absolute minimum; all of it contained in one medium backpack (around 45 litres for those who care about such things) and one small backpack (for day use) which just about fitted inside the bigger one.

Kit List

Torch	Cap	Walking boots	Travellers cheques
Batteries	Cotton trousers	Shoes	Passport
Penknife	Jogging bottoms	Sleeping bag	Tickets
Music	Shirt	Scarf	Insurance
Medical kit	Polo Shirt	Sweatshirt	Books
Wash kit	T-shirts × 3	Cagoule	
Sun block	Shorts × 4	Towel	
Shades	Socks × 4	Money	

It was perhaps debatable whether a pack of plasters, a bandage and some Germolene qualified as a medical kit but I felt I would be able to deal with most emergencies with these basics. The 'sleeping bag' was a scabby polycotton sheet which I had acquired from Help the Aged for 50p and then sewn into a cocoon shape with yellow cotton; useful for keeping off bugs at night and avoiding whatever alien life-forms may be inhabiting the mattresses of the lesser Indonesian guest house. And you never know when you might need a harmonica. Having the right kit for the job was clearly important.

My life was now reduced to 18 kilos of personal items and the contents of my head.

Travel

. . . not to go anywhere, but to go

The check-in queue. Centuries of human creativity is reduced to blank expressions and the shifting of weight from one foot to the other; fifty million years of evolution and we are no more than slightly morbid molluscs carrying our homes at our side. My particular queue consisted of:

1 – spotty German twelve-year-old with heavy trunk and overbearing mother engaged in animated discussion with woman behind counter about excess baggage;

2 – slightly scruffy 30 year old, tall and handsome, carrying battered red and blue backpack;

3 – gaunt businessman adorned with mobile phone and shiny briefcase.

My bus had arrived at Heathrow an hour after check-in time but having sprinted to Terminal Two it didn't seem to matter that I was late and I made a mental note never to rush to arrive on time in the future; a lesson that four weeks in Indonesia would reinforce.

Whilst the overbearing mother spluttered alternately at the increasingly red-faced child and the mannequin behind the desk, I amused myself by counting the number of times the businessman, who was clearly in disagreement with someone on the other end of his phone, said the word 'nine'. He made it to eight and then said 'Ja' – I was gutted.

As the overbearing mother spluttered in the distance I deposited my backpack, took my tickets and made my way to Departures wondering why the handrails on escalators moved faster than the escalator itself.

Standing in line for the X-ray machine, I watched the black rubbery flaps swallowing up my bag and waited with a feeling of guilt and trepidation that would only be justified if I was a drug dealer, urban terrorist or occasional hijacker of commercial airliners.

I wandered to the departure gate, feebly attempting to make myself inconspicuous amongst the pride of German businessmen decorated with mobile phones and shiny briefcases; feeling under-dressed I skulked onto the plane and found my window seat.

I was given the choice of a free copy of the *Daily Mail*, *Daily Telegraph* or *Die Somethingorother* – the German paper was probably the liberal alternative but I couldn't help but admire the irony of the other two promoting themselves on European business flights. Being linguistically challenged I took the Telegraph and reminded myself for an hour why I never read it.

Frankfurt airport was the same as any other except the drinks machine wouldn't accept my money. I had two hours to wait for my connection and so my diary began.

Thirty and bored. Work okay but not very satisfying; social life pretty good but too many friends and acquaintances getting old before their time – look into virus which apparently causes you to turn into a pumpkin if you stay at a nightclub past midnight; several failed or never-to-be relationships. Need a change, need to do something interesting and exciting, love SE-Asia, always wanted to see a volcano, absolutely nothing stopping me, and now I've got a ten hour overnight flight in front of me – shit.

It's nice to be privileged enough to have angst; to be in a relatively well-paid job with an all right house and an okay life and decide it's not what you want. But you've got to be careful with your soul; it doesn't suddenly go, you don't suddenly lose it. It quietly drifts away, piece by piece, in increments. You're lucky if you realise it. And you're lucky if you can do something about it.

I was happy with my window seat. We left Frankfurt in the evening and as I flicked through the pictures in my Lonely Planet the constellations of towns and villages below us looked alternately like butterflies, mythical creatures or Indonesian shadow puppets.

I was seated next to a nice Dutch couple (sounds like something your mum would say) who were bound for Malaysia – I now learnt the flight was landing in Kuala Lumpur first. We didn't really speak for the first hour but I'd guessed they weren't German because of the guttural noises they made from time to time which I was sure wasn't catarrh. Their book on Malaysia enabled me to make some pithy comment and then share my wisdom and knowledge. This was further sparked by their stated plan to go to Kota Bahru – a lovely little town on the east coast of which I had very fond memories (and now I sound like EM Forster's mum). I told them about the food, recommended a guest house which I believe was called the Windmill and told them about the utterly gorgeous Perentian islands. I had visited them in 1994 after hearing about their beauty from three Danish travellers who had been on a boat ferrying tourists which had capsized. Several people had died in the stormy seas and they had survived by clinging to wreckage for hours until they were rescued. Consequently the islands were deserted and I spent a very happy week there with the few who had made the journey; most of the time spent either in a hammock or playing guitar in the local bar. Would I go back? It's never the same.

After the talk of travel we covered various topics of mutual interest: the single currency (with which they seemed perfectly happy), the Dutch ability at mastering languages and the arrogance of the British. We inevitably got onto the subject of football and I discourteously reminded them of England's victory over Holland 4-1 in Euro '96 – this seemed to be less engrained in their collective memories. Apparently the important thing for Holland is beating the Germans – it's amazing how much common ground nations can have.

I tried to grab some sleep but being six feet tall in economy class is conducive to this in the same way that having a javelin through your neck is conducive to pirouetting in a particularly narrow corridor; five hours later I felt like shit – but I philosophically decided that it was all part of the wonder of travel.

If there isn't a book on aeroplane etiquette, there should be. Public transport is one of the few places where we tolerate strangers rubbing the outside of their thighs against our own – often whilst wearing shorts. And what is it with people who find it impossible to sit down without grabbing the seat in front of them (always mine). And what are the rules on who gets to put their elbows on the arm-rest?

On a 747, for example, you have three seats by the window but only four arm-rests. It doesn't take an anthropologist to know that, on average, three people have six arms – usually two each. Should two people have one arm each, or one person have no arms, then the seating design for the left and right sections of 747s would be spot on[2]; however, as it is statistically unlikely for this to happen, where should one put one's arms?

Tiring of ergonomics, I read my Lonely Planet guide to Java. On my last trip I had decided to go without a book on the dubious premise that the bloke who wrote it didn't have one, so why should I? It worked out better than it probably should have done and as I had three months to get around, the odd cock-up wasn't a problem. This time I had less than a month so planning seemed more important. I thought it might be appropriate to learn a little of

---

2 Though this, of course, would depend on the order in which the people were sitting, i.e. the person with no arms would have to sit in the middle – this would also mean one less person grabbing the seat in front when they got up and down.

the language. It stretched to and was pretty much confined by 'how much' (*berapa*) and 'thank you' (*terima kasih*), but what more do you need? In addition to this I also gained a basic grasp of Indonesian history which seemed to revolve around various power struggles involving Buddhists, Hindus, Muslims, the Portuguese, the Dutch, the British, the Japanese, independence, President Suharto and others. I hoped to learn more.

I said farewell to my Dutch friends and started the final leg of the journey on the deserted plane. Now I was finally going to make my trip over the equator – it was pointed out to me later that I was possibly the first member of my family to go to the Southern Hemisphere, which seemed quite remarkable. I expected the pilot to make an announcement as we crossed and I had prepared a witty piece of fiction about people desperately peering out of the window for the white line (or running white lion as someone once told me). I even considered asking to go into the cockpit for the occasion but decided I was too cool and too English for such an act of childish excitement – shame really but in retrospect it probably wasn't worth it due to the potential effort involved in convincing them that it wasn't just a ruse to enable me to hijack the plane with some liquid Germolene and a particularly pointy pen. As it happened there was no announcement and I was left vainly peering out of the window for some sign.

We eventually landed at 5:30 local time. I wandered through the tidy corridors of the airport and reached the immigration queue still not feeling as excited as I should. I guess this was due to some trepidation about what on earth Jakarta was like, would I catch the right bus and would I find somewhere to stay?

Immigration was the usual cheerful bundle of laughs.

Immigration Training Manual

Section 2 – Client contact

1 – Take passport in brisk manner.

2 – On no account smile or establish eye contact.

3 – Take out small and complicated white immigration form on which tourist has given detail normally only required for joining national security services, and discard.

4 – Speak to a colleague – about something related or unrelated.

5 – Pause with some degree of dramatic effect.

6 – Stamp passport on completely random page.

7 – Place passport on counter in slightly flippant manner.

8 – On no account smile or establish eye contact.

I stood in the random lottery of the baggage hall waiting for my backpack, experiencing that anticipation of Christmas Eve when you're wondering what Santa will bring in the full knowledge that it could quite easily be someone else's cast-offs. I got what I wanted and wandered through customs, who had decided that all bags needed to be X-rayed, and here I was. The arrival hall was as busy as any other arrival hall. Less shops than in the West and more dark skin but otherwise unremarkable. I prepared myself for the expected onslaught of conmen, rip-off merchants, murderers and sundry other characters who would vie for my attention and I put on my "I'm really confident and know where I'm going" look.

I looked around for a moneychanger (avoiding the persistent calls for taxis), as I had been unable to obtain currency in the UK; apparently the banks had been unwilling to hold stocks of rupiah due to its rapid descent to the value of monopoly money. In just two years that rate had crashed from £1 = 4,000Rp to £1 = 18,000Rp ($1 = 13,000Rp), the effect of which had been massive rises in the cost of Indonesian imports and economic calamity. On the positive side it made me really rich. The money changers were offering atrocious rates and I received 30% less than I expected – 10,000Rp for my one-dollar travellers cheques (but when you're talking that kind of money who cares).

I questioned the 'Information' counter about the cheap 4,000Rp (25p) Damri airport bus to the city centre and was waved in a vague direction. I was then quickly surrounded by a throng of taxi drivers, people offering to show me the way (for money or kindness?), people enquiring after my health ("Meesster. How are yooou? Wheh are you going?"), and a man trying to sell me perfume for my wife (maybe if I'd asked he would have introduced me to her). I found the bus stop and waited with some locals in the early evening humidity, as inconspicuous as a blind man's stick in a cup of coffee.

The bus soon arrived and I was followed on by a couple who sat down behind me. As the only Westerners I had seen since landing I thought I ought to say "Hi". In backpacking terms this tends to be less about sociability and more about exchanging information. It's an opportunity to pick up tips on where they've been and hopefully where you're going; it's someone to share a taxi with; it's someone to watch your bags; it's someone with whom you can offload all your politically incorrect thoughts about your frustrations with the locals; it's someone to share your life story with; and perhaps sometimes it's someone who you might meet up with again once in your life. There are people I have met for six hours who know more about me than people I have known for six years – a bit like being stuck in a lift I guess.

At some point I learnt they were called Christopher and Castella (I think). They had also both been travelling before but it was their first time in Indonesia. Their English was patchy, but a) my French is worse; and b) once again our European cousins can speak our language even though they've never been to the UK.

We agreed that once we got to the central Gambir railway station we could go to Jalan Jaksa, the backpacking area, together.

The trip into Jakarta was good and the opulent tree-lined route was impressive – where was the evidence of political and economic crisis? On arrival at the station we were accosted by a clamour of taxi drivers but decided the fee of 25,000Rp was extortionate. Using the tall monument in Merdeka Square to navigate by, plus the Lonely Planet map, we decided to take the ten minute walk to Jalan Jaksa. It turned into twenty minutes as we failed our basic map-reading test and had to avoid very large holes in the pavement, but it gave us time to chat and make me thankful for packing relatively lightly. I didn't think it was too hot but by the time we reached the first guest house my back was soaking.

Jalan Jaksa was an average street in an average part of the city. A collection of guest houses and restaurants lined the road in a similar way to the backpackers' heaven (or purgatory?) of Khao San Road in Bangkok but ten percent of the size.

We were beckoned into Wisma Delima, a grubby and tired family-run place, had a look round, 15,000Rp single and 20,000Rp double, but decided to explore further. A mad looking man with a comedy limp grabbed us 100 metres down the road and took us up an alleyway to Bloom Steem hostel quoting the same prices. It was clean, plainly tiled and quiet but they wanted to charge me 20,000Rp as they had no singles left. Christopher and Castella were happy but I decided to amicably stand my ground at 15,000Rp. At this point I was told to go elsewhere then – they weren't supposed to say that. I decided if I left they would call me back so I started walking. Really slowly. Waiting for the call. Nobody followed. So much for my haggling skills.

Within a minute I was caught by a small, smiling bald man, who took me down three alleyways to his house. He was extremely nice and the place was cheap but there was no-one else staying there. I wasn't happy with leaving my bags completely unattended when I went out so I made my excuses and wandered back to Bloom Steem. I walked in grinning as magnanimously as possible and took my 20,000Rp room – pointless squabbling over 30p really.

After a quick shower I met with C and C and we checked out the local eateries. Standard backpacker behaviour when getting to a new town – find a room, get some food. We went into the busiest place, generally a good sign, and grabbed a wooden bench and table looking onto the road; the satay and fresh papaya juice were just what I needed. After a while we realised that there was a limit to the number of conversations we could have in patchy English and decided it was time for bed; it was 10pm here and 3pm in England, but of course I hadn't slept. We said *bon nuit* and I was asleep before I got to my room.

Brief Encounters
(one day in Jakarta)

Lain ladang,
lain belalang

Waking up alone in a strange town. The room seemed like a cell and the only noise was the phut-phut-phut of the fan moving the warm air around and the occasional echoes of foreign voices floating down the corridors of the hotel. It was outrageously early and I ate breakfast alone. By 8:00 I was trudging the broad, characterless streets. So this was Jakarta, the centre of power for a nation of over 200,000,000 people; a city which had witnessed extreme breakdowns of law and order and violent riots on the streets. It was quiet today.

For over thirty years power had resided with President Suharto but corruption, ethnic strife, economic collapse and political unrest had brought an end to that in 1998. Billions of dollars had been flowing out of the country as the world realised that the huge loans it had given to the government and to Indonesian companies had been wasted through corruption and poor management. An economic crisis had increased the unhappiness of sections of the population who were frustrated with the lack of political choice under their authoritarian system of government; 'guided democracy' as it was euphemistically called. Election campaigning was so restricted that the government party, Golkar, was guaranteed to win, largely helped by the silencing of dissidents by such subtle means as torture and jail sentences of up to 13 years. Tensions had increased to the extent that pro-democracy demonstrators had clashed with security forces in several cities and in one incident more than 120 people had died in a shopping centre set alight by rioters.

I jumped as a man rattled up the shutters of a camera shop on the other side of the road. I carried on walking.

The knock-on effect had been a rise in ethnic tension and there had been attacks by mainly Muslim crowds on Christian churches, Buddhist temples and shops owned by ethnic Chinese Indonesians. A once tolerant country had been pushed into conflict by popular resentment over the growing gap between rich and poor, and the corruption of officialdom. An outbreak of violence had occurred in West Kalimantan, Borneo, where disagreements between the local Dyak people and Muslim immigrants from the Island of Madura had escalated into extreme violence. Large groups of Dyaks, armed with machetes and rifles, had attacked Madurese communities and many of the Madurese were beheaded, with some reports of cannibalism. At least 1,000 people were thought to have died, and whole villages had been burned to the ground. Unrest in East Timor had been exacerbated by an increase in abuses of the local population by the Indonesian military and there had been an upsurge of activity by pro-independence rebels.

Another featureless block. 1960s concrete by the look of it. But very clean streets.

And then there was the impact of *El Nino* weather patterns which had resulted in much of the country experiencing the worst drought in living memory.

As his political support withered away and mass demonstrations increased, Suharto was forced to resign and power was given to his crony, Habibie, with a 'promise' of economic and political reform. His reign lasted a year as the 1998 Indonesian Revolution finally led to open and free elections but the promised 'reformasi' continued to be slow as corruption, a weak economy and ethnic tension held back change. At the dawn of the new millennium Jakarta was holding its breath.

"Hello, sir," was the cheerful salutation from two guys on their way to somewhere. I smiled.

I wandered down to the railway station in order to buy a ticket for that evening's train to Yogyakarta. Java was a large island and I would have to carefully pick what I was going to explore if I was to be able to take in Bali and Lombok. Yogyakarta was a main city to the south-west and the cultural centre of Java; from there I could see the ancient temples and major volcanoes of the area. Thankfully there was a decent train link – always preferable over the Russian Roulette that is road travel in this part of the world.

It seemed to be a quiet morning at the station. A small group of young men dressed smartly in white shirts and beige trousers were chatting at the entrance as I slid into the grey tiled interior. A young woman in a red T-shirt, black trousers and waistcoat was leaning against one of the yellow columns silently observing the to and fro of people around her; people whose hair colour may have been similar but who were part of country consisting of around 300 ethnic groups – Javanese, Sundanese, Malay, Chinese and many others. A mix of dialects, customs and religions all attempting to live under the national motto of 'unity in diversity' – and trying to sort out a train journey at the same time.

I found the timetables and eventually figured out the journey I wanted. Now I had to buy the ticket. I asked the information desk and when it didn't answer, I asked the small man behind it whose head I could just see over the top. It transpired that he was actually just sitting down but it provided me with some amusement. He told me that the booth opened at 3pm but suggested I arrived at 2pm as it could be busy and I didn't want to be standing for the ten hour journey – a good point, I thought.

I decided to take some photos. This encouraged a small cheerful boy in a big pink T-shirt who should have been selling newspapers to spend his time jumping up and down in front of me. It eventually seemed easier to ask him to be in the photo and so I took a picture of his beaming face, much to the amusement of the surrounding audience. I walked out to Merdeka Square towards the 132 metre high Monas monument – a national phallus with a flame on top. It was a pretty vacant space with none of the atmosphere of, say, Sanam Luang, the area in front of the Grand Palace in Bangkok, which is very much a place for the people; it just seemed like an expensive example of misguided government extravagance. Two middle-aged women in pink trousers and tops flagged me down and insisted I take their picture as they sat regally on the grass with two bottles of vegetable oil and some plastic bags full of shopping. Some bored government workers (in what looked like yellow pyjamas) then did the same and as a queue began to form I felt it was time to bid a hasty farewell. Past the intermittent postcard sellers I walked to one of the main shopping streets, Jalan Thamin and a large shopping centre complete with KFC and McDonald's. It was heart-warming to see that these worthy examples of homogenised global culture (and I don't mean yoghurt) had spread to a country with such a diverse and fascinating history. Full of shops but lacking in customers I wandered around the empty mall, occasionally catching the eye of impassive shop assistants. It was approaching 11:00 and as I needed to check out at 12:00 I wandered back to the guest house.

No sign of C and C, I rested, packed and deposited my backpack at reception for 'safekeeping' (sitting in the hallway with a sign on it saying "please take me"). With a couple of hours to kill there seemed to be a lack of things to see or do and I found myself in a department store looking at brightly coloured shirts, cheap toys and sweet-smelling wooden boxes. In the basement was a food court where, surreally, there was a band of wandering minstrels moving unmelodiously between the plastic chairs and tables. Their set list seemed to be restricted to dubious covers of Western hits from the sixties and seventies and also what I assumed to be local chart stuff, which sounded like the songs that failed to make the short-list for the Latvian entry in the Eurovision song contest. They appeared to be taking requests and as much as I liked the idea of hearing their very own brand of 'Bohemian Rhapsody', I decided to quietly order some chicken satay instead.

My cabaret lunch completed I walked out into the hot afternoon towards the train station. This would have been an uneventful journey had it not been for a rather odd experience with a becak driver. The three-wheeled bicycle with its canopy-covered passenger bench at the front can be seen in most Indonesian towns, and walking down a quiet side road, I heard the quiet whirr of the becak behind me. I waited for the offer of transport that I knew would be forthcoming and subconsciously began to walk faster. The call came.

"Transport?"

The question had the same inflection as you or I asking it, the only difference being that in Indonesia the 'tran' is pronounced in a Liverpudlian accent but often with a rolled 'r' and the 'sport', as well as going up a key or two, is spoken very quickly. I shook my head and the driver continued on his way for a short while. He then slowed down in order to ride behind me and then continued just in front of me. His head was turned in my direction but instead of further requests for business he just looked at my shorts with an odd expression on his face. He almost seemed to be looking at my crotch but I decided that would be just too strange and guessed that perhaps he was just vaguely amused at a Westerner walking around in shorts (something the locals can find childish or scruffy depending on the occasion). This, accompanied with the occasional point of his finger, continued for a couple of minutes until we got to the end of the road. I was intending to go straight on but suddenly the becak driver accelerated, cut in front of me, reached out with his hand, grabbed my genitals and drove off with a broad smile.

Pervert or bizarre Javanese welcome? Further time in Java confirmed the likelihood of the former. However, there's a saying in Indonesia – go to a different place and you will find different people and different customs; they put it much more succinctly though – *lain ladang, lain belalang* – different field, different grasshopper. There were certainly a few different grasshoppers around.

I arrived at the station at 2:25 and a small queue had developed. I sat cross-legged on the station floor behind a guy with floppy dark hair pushed back by a pair of fake Ray-Bans. With a big smile he introduced himself as Banja and told me he had just returned from a town in the north where he worked in a hospital. He was off to Jogya (slang for Yogyakarta, rhymes with Roger) with his girlfriend to see family. We talked about the economy, politics, life in Indonesia, and I was interested by how happy he was to be openly scathing about Suharto and the previous regime.

He pointed at a crest which looked like an eagle with a shield.

"You know this?" he asked.

I shook my head.

"Pancasila," he said. "National symbol of Indonesia."

There were five principles, he explained, on which the country was founded: Faith in God (any God); Humanity (the unity of mankind); Nationalism (rather than ethnic differences); Representative government (based on consensus); Social justice (including adequate food and clothing for all).

He seemed proud of this. Much of what was happening in Indonesia seemed to be the antithesis of these principles but he was happy to recognise the faults of the country's economic and political systems and yet still retain an undiminished pride in his nation; this became a recurring theme for the rest of the trip.

The ticket booth eventually opened and as I was standing in line I was approached by an American guy who told me he was living in Sumatra in a small village. He impressed me with the way in which he had "got down with the locals" and how it was "much better than LA, man", and after what seemed like an eternity it was me at the front of the queue.

I wanted to catch the 8:40pm train arriving at 5:15am and I wanted to travel executive class as I felt I could afford to upgrade from business (36,000Rp to 76,000Rp). Saying '*executif*' wasn't a problem, but when I said '*delapan*' meaning 'eight' in order to signify the 8:40pm rather than the 7:20pm train, the man got very confused. How he couldn't understand my elaborate conception and execution of the language I shall never know. He considered offering me eight tickets but with the appropriate hand signals and the occasional bout of pointing we eventually came to an agreement and I got what I wanted.

I took the now well-trodden route back to the guest house and got chatting to a blond-haired English guy in a cream baseball cap who wandered past me in the reception area. His name was Jon and he had just come from Australia. We wandered over to the restaurant opposite, which curiously seemed to have modelled itself on a 17th century English inn, and sat down at one of the dark wooden tables. Around us were a few travellers, all beads and tie-dye, some local girls and a few Indo-Chinese businessmen. We shared stories for the rest of the afternoon and he was particularly animated about his experiences in the infamous nightclub, Tanamur, and its mix of locals, expats, prostitutes, pimps and lady-boys. He had gone there the previous evening but was most put out that he'd bought a local girl drinks all night and she had left with another guy. It seems the path of true love never runs smoothly.

We decided to grab some food and chatted over a leisurely two hour dinner which cost £1 each. During the course of the meal a note arrived on the table.

Hello my name is Rui. Get to the poins I like you very much and want you come join us.

We looked over at the local girls, trying to work out which one it was and then tried to compose a witty response; after ten minutes I realised it was time to get the train and so left Jon to it. I wonder if they married.

I arrived half an hour early with an air of nervous anticipation and was pointed to the right platform by a helpful guard. This, of course, didn't stop me asking three other people on the way, two of which were on the train. Executive class was a long carriage with pairs of white plastic seats down either side which could slide to 30 degrees for sleeping. It seemed to be dominated by slightly overweight forty-something businessmen in pink shirts. The diesel-engined *kereta api* (cart of fire) dragged us out of Gambir station into the dark evening and soon the state railway's hostesses were bringing us dinner (something in sauce) and taking our drinks orders (coffee or water). We were then given blankets and the opportunity to hire a pillow.

I had very little sleep as we rattled our way across central Java through sleeping towns, past plantations of soybeans and palm oil, and within sight of massive volcanoes – all hidden by the deep night. I also seemed to acquire a number of small bites but the nine hours wasn't as bad as I thought it might be and the implausibly pink sky at 5:30 almost made up for any discomfort.

I prepared myself for the expected scrum at Jogya station and tightened my backpack as I stepped from the train. I walked with the crowd towards an onslaught of taxi drivers trying to charge obscene amounts (25p) for the short journey to the guest houses and marched purposefully through the thronging masses with the intention of finding a place called the Losmen something-or-other. I was quickly accosted by a guy who wanted to show me his guest house.

"I'm looking for Losmen..." I said.

"Yes. Yes," He replied.

Excellent. He knew of it. I followed him across the road and down an alleyway to a tidy looking place.

"This is Losmen?" I asked.

"Yes. Yes," he said with a confused look.

That was lucky. I'd found the one I wanted.

How was I supposed to know that *losmen* was the generic word for guest house?

But the Losmen Prashah Jaya was fine for 8,000Rp – double bed, fan, and clean. I threw my bags on the floor, had a shower and fell asleep.

Games, Frames and Automobiles
(Yogyakarta)

Caveat emptor

It was now Sunday lunchtime. The corridors of the guest house were quiet but the low table just outside my room had acquired a cup, a small container of sugar, some ants and a plastic flask of tea. I decided to get some food and wandered out into the daylight, along a couple of alleyways and into a restaurant where I ordered a traditional Sunday lunch (noodle soup). I had managed to find my way to the Jalan Sosro part of Jogya, a main backpacking area, complete with numerous guest houses, restaurants and tiny shops. Yet I was the only one here. No bum bags, nobody carefully perusing a shiny copy of Lonely Planet, no "So how long have you been travelling then?"; a whole place set up for backpackers – empty.

But life was continuing outside my guest house. Nestling amongst the narrow alleyways was an open dusty play area which I had briefly spotted, empty and tired, at 6:00 this morning. It was now full of excitement and I found my way to the guest house's roof to watch the events that were taking place. A piece of cord was suspended across the width of the area with five or six pieces of string with hooks on them hanging from it. Small children with big smiles stood under each one wearing a classic straw 'coolie' hat with a ring in the top. Behind them were approximately thirty kids, assorted parents, loud music, and a man with a microphone controlling affairs; the winner being the one who was first to hook the hat without using their hands.

They were clearly having a brilliant time as laughter and shouts of encouragement mixed with the music and bounced off the walls. Backpacking often has the feel of sneaking backstage at a show, capturing those events that the people in the expensive seats never get to see – you may lose some of the stage-managed glamour but you get much more of the excitement.

I watched the fun for a while (I think the winner was a pretty girl in a Manchester United away strip) took some photos and started chatting to a local who had wandered up onto the roof behind me. He told me that this week was a special week when lots of activities were organised for the local kids and today was silly games day.

His name was Ecu, tall and in his 20s, casually dressed in jeans, T-shirt and the ubiquitous flip-flops. He spoke very good English, asking me about my travels and telling me about the various trips I could take in the area. I told him about my interest in music and he told me about a man who made guitars – this I was interested in.

We agreed to speak again later and I decided to investigate the town. The wide Jalan Malioboro (Marlborough Street) ran through the centre of Jogya from the train station to the Sultan's Palace. Becaks, andongs (horse-drawn carriages) and motorbikes clamoured for space amongst the cars and lorries. Market stalls filled the pavements. T-shirts, belts, carvings, material, watches. My eye was caught by a Nike baseball cap so I decided to ask how much this fine piece of headware would cost.

"Berapa?"

The hat-man grinned and told me 20,000.

"Expensive, you give me good price," I said.

"How much you pay?"

"Ten thousand."

"No. Fifteen."

"No. Too much, ten good price." How could I be bitching over one pound, I asked myself.

"Okay. Twelve thousand."

"No, come on, ten thousand."

"Okay, meester."

I couldn't believe it. It was too easy. Was I the King of Hagglers or had I just been done? Regardless, I had just acquired a very nice baseball cap for 50p.

Further on down the road, I was stopped by a man in smart trousers and short-sleeved shirt who greeted me with a broad smile.

"Hello meester, how are you?"

"Very well, thank you."

"Where you from?"

"England," I replied. I had learned that Britain or the UK was a concept many people had trouble understanding out here.

"Ah, England, very good. Lady Dee. How long you stay here?"

"I've just arrived."

"Oh, you've seen batik?"

"A little bit."

"Oh we have special show on today, very good batik."

"That's good but I'm not really interested, I'm at the beginning of my holiday, maybe another time."

"Oh no, last day of show today we give special discount, you come see."

"Well like I said I'm not interested in buying anything..."

"Oh no problem, you come see."

I could feel myself getting sucked into a situation which I knew I wanted to avoid but a little bit of tiredness on my part and friendly persuasion on his part meant that the next thing I knew I was walking down a series of quiet alleyways to this 'special show'.

We arrived at the 'gallery' – two large rooms with various pieces of the richly-coloured fabric hanging on every spare bit of wall space; some of it framed, some it hanging free.

Another guy greeted me with a smooth salesman's smile.

"You want tea?" he asked, pouring me a cup.

Seems I do, I thought, as he handed it to me.

"No problem, you just looking."

I wandered around and politely looked at the some of the examples of beach scenes and agricultural scenes.

"I am artist," said the smooth guy.

"Really?" I said in a "yeah and I could be your long lost brother but it's unlikely" kind of way.

"You know how to make?" he asked, and before waiting for a reply he pulled out a metre long piece of fabric and demonstrated how the wax was put on and explained how it was then dyed.

"It's very nice," I told him as I struggled to come up with a getaway plan, "but like I said I don't really want anything at the moment. Heavy bag, too much too carry."

"Oh no, not heavy," they replied in unison.

Come on, Nick, sort it out.

"You like this one?" he asked, pointing at a blue and black agricultural scene I had been looking at.

"It's very nice," I replied.

"How much you pay?"

"I don't want to buy, thank you."

"Price two hundred and fifty dollars, we give you special price one hundred dollars."

I laughed out loud at this ridiculous price.

"Okay, how much you pay?"

"No, really, I'm not interested."

"No, how much you pay?"

"I'm sorry, I'm at beginning of holiday, have little money, student, don't really want."

"Okay. Okay. Forty dollars. Last price."

"No, really, thank you."

"How much you pay?"

"Look, if you had something for around fifty thousand Rupiah[3] I may be interested," I said, hoping that they didn't, "but really I don't want anything."

"Okay. Okay. Ten dollars. Last price."

Blimey, I thought – it's supposed to cost $250.

"Look," I said. "I haven't got any money now anyway, so let me have a think about it and I'll come back if I'm interested."

"No special day, gone tomorrow," they said, covering the doorway.

"Okay. What time are you going this evening?

"Very soon."

"Okay, well I might come back later," I said, edging around them and towards the door.

"Hey, special price today. Very good."

"Yes, I know," I replied. "Thank you very much it was nice to see your work."

I stepped out of the shop and walked quickly up the alleyway, trying to remember the way I'd come and hoping they weren't following me. I could here the noise of Jalan Malioboro and was happy to set eyes on its welcoming clouds of carbon monoxide. Thankfully that little excursion hadn't turned nasty but I knew better than to get into those situations. Rule number one: Don't go wandering off with strange men just because they're nice to you.

I crossed the busy road to the main mall, passed the insidious McDonalds and looked at the cheap T-shirts, Levis, CDs and cheap prescription glasses. A Western girl in the opticians told me that they should cost around £30 and the eye test was free – so much for the great British National Health Service. A free Indonesian eye test sounded interesting so I agreed to purchase some glasses and was

---

3 Around $5

led into a little back room. Disappointingly there was no dubious looking equipment or scary bits of machinery and the test was carried out with the minimum of fuss in exactly the same way as it would be anywhere. I was told they would be ready within 48 hours and walked out into the stuffy afternoon.

On my way back to the guest house I bumped into Ecu hanging out on a street corner and he took me to his brother's travel agents (wooden shack) to arrange a trip to the ancient Buddhist temple of Borobudur and Hindu temples of Prambanan. Hidden from the Western World for centuries, I was keen to discover them for myself and had planned to attempt to take the public transport route; the sunrise trip for 15,000Rp, however, seemed a good option and so I agreed to do that. We then went to see the guitar man with his made-to-order guitars.

One hundred metres up Jalan Sosro was a row of low buildings and in one of them was a small, cheerful man, balding, with a squint, who made guitars. He reminded me of the shopkeeper in the children's TV programme 'Mr Benn', except he didn't wear a fez, or hire out costumes. He had a tiny workshop next to his tiny living room with a couple of guitars on the wall and a collection of semi-made bodies. He brought out a couple of finished acoustics which in England would have cost around £150. I briefly played them and then looked at his 'catalogue' which was a collection of photographs ripped from old music magazines of a range of different styles. Using Ecu as a translator he told me he could make anything I wanted and that the price was 400,000Rp (£20) or 500,000Rp with an electric pickup. A fantastic price, but if I wanted one specially made it would take two weeks and I would have to come back to Jogya to pick it up – I said I'd need to think about it.

I then made a quick visit to an international telephone place as I thought I ought to check in with home, had dinner and returned to the hotel. The trip was leaving at 5am so I set the alarm for 4:51 as that was plenty enough time to get ready at that time of day. Five days earlier I wouldn't have conceived of getting up at such a satanic hour. I went to bed.

Nirvana
(discovering temples)

He who recites Ramayana
should have rich gifts of cows and gold

I awoke at 2:00 thinking it was 4:00 but eventually got back to sleep. The house cockerel started at 3:30. At 4:30 I had a five minute call to prayer just outside my window. Five minutes later there was a knock at the door – they had assumed I would need a wake-up call. I was with the minibus by 4:50.

A guy with short, brown, wavy hair and glasses was snoozing in the back.

"Hi," I greeted him.

"Hi." From his voice I assumed him to be English but later found out he was Scottish. His name was Mike. The only other tourist was a Japanese girl whose name I forgot, so we'll call her Suki. The young Indonesian guide introduced himself as Andy.

It really was an atrocious time to be up but Mike and I started chatting. He was on a pretty major round the world tour and on his way to Australia to work; the world of investment banking in London had proved a poor substitute for a year spent negotiating the price of bus transport and trying to get the best deal on a room with a fan. He was particularly tired as he had been to see the erupting Merapi volcano the night before.

"What do you mean it's erupting?"

"It's erupting."

"I was going to climb it."

"You'll have a job."

This sounded fantastic. We chatted for the whole of the forty-five minute journey and arrived at Borobudur as it was getting light.

Borobudur, over a millennium old, was buried under volcanic ash for hundreds of years until it was rediscovered by Stamford Raffles in the 19th Century and took its place as one of the great wonders of the world. I had little idea of what to expect and was impatient to get through the large iron gates that blocked the entrance to this hidden marvel.

We were admitted at 6:00 and with the rest of the early-rising pilgrims, took the manicured walkway to the temple. As we rounded the corner the sheer vastness of it hit us. Terrace upon terrace floating in the morning mist. Numerous levels emerging from a base 123 metres wide; carefully shaped stonework rising metaphorically, if not literally to Nirvana. I tried to imagine what it must have been like for pilgrims a thousand years ago, struck with awe at the size of the place; and then how Raffles must have felt when he realised what he had found.

We strode through the cool morning air expecting the apparition in front of us to disappear at any minute. Reaching its high grey walls, we took one of the four stone stairways and set out for the top. Sunrise was fast approaching and so rather than take the correct clockwise Buddhist route around the various levels, we moved quickly up the steep steps, passing through intricately carved stone gateways. The top was breathtaking – the architecture of the temple (built around 800 AD) with its dozens of stupas (bell-shaped shrines), and the incredible panoramic views of lush vegetation, towering volcanic cliffs and rolling clouds of mist. The sunrise was all but obliterated by the clouds but this helped enhance the serene atmosphere; despite the dozen or so who were congregated at the top there was nothing but hushed voices and quiet contemplation.

The surrounding countryside changed with the light and rolling mist. When the sun finally appeared it cut long shadows and turned everything into a perfect photograph.

Eventually day fully arrived and I wandered around Nirvana appreciating the work that must have gone into it. The upper part of the temple consisted of three circular terraces covered by seventy-two 4 metre high stupas with one massive stupa at the top. All but the central one had a stone Buddha inside, deep in meditation behind the lattice stone-work. Conveniently, one of the stupas had disappeared over time revealing a serene stone Buddha in the lotus position.

For over an hour I took in the magical atmosphere and then slowly wandered down to look at each of the square terraces. The carvings along the stone walls were incredibly intricate; the upper levels representing man's effort to achieve ultimate enlightenment and the lower levels showing a corrupt world dominated by passion and covetousness. Events from the life of Gautama Siddhartha (Buddha) were depicted, as were scenes from eighth century Javanese life: merchants, warriors, ships, elephants, dancing girls, musicians. Strange gargoyle-type creatures stared out at me, successfully warding off evil spirits; and four hundred buddhas sat impassively on the walls, their faces towards the forest and volcanoes that surrounded them, their minds serenely oblivious to this.

What was even more astonishing was that Borobudur shouldn't have still been here. It had suffered from subsidence ever since it had been built and much of the carved stonework had been damaged by erosion since it had been dug out of the volcanic ash that had covered it for centuries. However, a restoration project started by a Dutch engineer at the beginning of the twentieth century was eventually finished by an incredible partnership between the Indonesian government and UNESCO who moved and reconstructed over a million stone blocks.

I walked around the base and looked back at the interplay of stone and sky. A journey through life: desire to form to formlessness. It was a remarkable place.

I took some last shots and as it was approaching 8:00 I began to wander back to the meeting place. I was immediately accosted by a gaggle of hawkers (is that the collective noun?) trying to sell me buddhas, photos and postcards. One particularly insistent man followed me a full two hundred metres, bargaining with me the whole way. I got him down from 10,000Rp to 1,000Rp by simply saying: 'no, sorry, I have photo, I don't want' around thirty times. He seemed to think that I was adopting some kind of cunning bargaining position but in reality I just didn't want his bloody postcards. Eventually he relented.

I joined Mike for the free breakfast of tea, toast and fruit and discovered that he had just had exactly the same experience. Thinking about it later I felt a bit guilty as I wondered how many sales he was making per day in the current economic climate; but I didn't want any postcards so what was I supposed to do- buy something from everyone who offered? I decided to develop a way to deal with this: from what point on I would buy things from people I like; an arbitrary system based on how I felt that day. Completely fair.

We left the small restaurant and were enthusiastically approached by an Indonesian family who wanted us to take a photo for them; except it transpired that they wanted a photo taken with them. Mike and I sandwiched ourselves between mum and dad with the four kids either side and we smiled at uncle as he took a couple of nice family snaps.

Back on the minibus I lay down for a quick snooze and Andy decided to start his earnest tour guide patter with a vengeance. I know it was all extremely interesting, but I just wanted to sleep. We arrived at the small Buddhist temple of Candi Mendut around ten minutes later – it was probably built earlier than Borobudur, was of a more Hindu-influenced style and had a wide three metre high stone Buddha within it. We were pounced upon by a number of old women as we attempted to enter the temple. They were selling everything from T-shirts to carvings; they also had a special range of things that went whizz along with bamboo that you could play 'Happy Birthday' on; and they were insistent. We ducked and dived and 1,000Rp bought us sanctuary in the temple compound.

Andy gave us detailed historical analysis of a number of nooks (but curiously no crannies) and I gave him my full attention by trying to take a picture of a skinny but fast-moving chicken. Once more we ducked and dived our way through the old women (some of them can really move) and we were safely back on the minibus. The beginning of our one and a half hour journey to Prambanan involved Andy giving us an explanation of the subtle differences of the Hindu and Buddhist faiths in a little bit too much detail. I nodded in the appropriate places, not having the heart to tell him that I knew the main stuff, was having real trouble getting around his syntax on the rest of it and was a bit tired; I'm not a good student in the morning. He then asked for questions from the floor and so in an attempt to change the subject to something less cerebrally-challenging I pointed to a paddy field and said: 'is that rice?' Andy then delighted in educating us about the finer points of ancient and modern agricultural processes in central Java – that'll teach me.

The early morning had caught up with all of us and we were worried that we might be a bit templed out; however, on reaching the Hindu temples of Prambanan, this quickly changed. Built around fifty years after Borobudur, the remains of around 240 temples had been found in this area. The main complex was an incredible sight, built from dark volcanic rock the temples were extremely imposing and the intricate detail was unbelievable. The towering central Shiva temple was 47 metres high, lavishly carved, and adorned with strange creatures. Smaller temples to Brahma and

Vishnu flanked it with other smaller shrines surrounding them. Scenes from the epic story of the Ramayana could be seen everywhere, Rama's wife, Sita, being abducted by Ravana, Hanuman the monkey-god, the fight to find and free her. In a place like this, you could happily believe it was all true as the stories and scenes were vividly brought back to life by craftsman over 1,000 years ago.

I wandered around admiring the architecture and looking for artistic camera angles to capture the size of the place. I'm not quite how I managed to bump into Suki around every corner but Mike ventured that she was stalking me and that I'd pulled. Obviously. Mike, however, had acquired his own stalker in the shape of a man from Kalimantan (Borneo) who found this curly-haired, beige creature extremely fascinating. I watched at an amused distance as he ushered Mike towards his family and jumped around taking a number of group photos. (Mental note: write jazz standard called 'Stan's the man from Kalimantan'.)

It was now approaching midday and the sun was beating down as loudly as it could so we ambled to the reception area and drank several bottles of coke. Suki chatted to us about her religion (Buddhism) and how much she had loved seeing these places and we were soon collected by Andy who took us back to the minibus. A short drive and we were deposited at a restaurant which had impressive views of the temple. Lunch was expensive chicken and rice, not particularly good and regularly interrupted by members of the Small Noisy Cat Club.

Suki wandered off for a walk leaving Mike and I to conclude that these were possibly the two most impressive temples in the world – certainly that we'd seen in south-east Asia – and that the Indonesian waitresses were very cute but how did these places get by when they were always overpopulated with staff with very little to do; and did they all get paid?

Suki returned from her walk and we chatted to Andy about his Muslim religion, how often he prayed, and his watch on which he had a compass so that he always knew which way Mecca was. He also informed us of how Indonesian men found Japanese women really attractive – we teased Suki and Andy about this for the rest of the journey home.

We arrived back in Jogya at 2:00 and arranged to meet at the oddly named Superman II restaurant at 8:00 that evening. I returned to the guest house and went straight to bed – for a man who can't sleep during the day I did remarkably well, waking up at around 5:00.

I wandered down to Jalan Malioboro but suddenly felt an overwhelming powerlessness and found myself sucked into McDonalds like Luke Skywalker into the Death Star. Against my will, I was forced to order a 15,000Rp Big Mac meal, expensive for the area but still only 75p; the locals also seemed to have temporarily gone to the dark side as the place was packed with most of them consuming McDonalds' special McFried Chicken and Rice meal. Having eaten, I felt sick as usual and wandered slowly to Superman II.

Mike turned up just after me and after an excellent ginseng coffee we decided to hunt for a restaurant that didn't serve burger and chips. We bumped into Ecu, always around when you needed him, who recommended Catherine's – it was just over the road so we checked out the menu and sat down. Not the best selection but the noodle soup was good. It was approaching 10pm when we paid the bill and we walked to the allegedly 'happening' Borobudur bar. The drinks were more expensive – as much as 70p for a large bottle of beer. We decided to try the Guinness but its promising appearance at our table disguised a dubious taste of ginger and coriander – exotic but not in a good way.

A local band was doing a selection of cover versions, 'No Woman No Cry', 'I Shot The Sheriff', etc. The lead singer was pretty good except he did that brilliant south-east Asian thing where you sing the vague sounds of words rather than the words themselves; quite what sentiments he was trying to express, therefore, I shall never know but I'm sure it wasn't precisely what Bob Marley intended. They stopped for a break and we realised that the video that had been playing in the background was Madonna in concert. It was obviously relatively recent and Mike had a minor rant about the amount of plastic surgery he thought she'd had. I clearly wasn't as *au fait* with this particular aspect of popular culture as him and I ended up paying more attention to what looked like dubious miming at a live gig.. She simulated sex for fifteen minutes and then our band came back on; we put up with them until 'Knocking On Heavens Door' (marmar, tek thees gurn offa meeee . . . nak, nak, nakking on heffen's dorrr, argh, argh, argh-argh, yeh) and decided to go and check out a local club.

I went back to my hotel to look at my map of Jogya and we then took the relatively long walk through the dark streets to what I hoped would be Papillon disco. We eventually found it but it looked extremely quiet. The large sign optimistically proclaimed that Monday night was ladies night. The entrance fee was 10,000Rp but Mike said he'd pop in and investigate first. He returned three minutes later saying that it was a bit empty but he'd met two Western guys at the bar (whom he decided were gay) who said it was an okay place. We paid our 50p which included a free soft drink and went in.

It was the darkest nightclub I had ever not seen. We tripped and stumbled to the bar and introduced ourselves to Roger and Dominic from Switzerland (who were only gay if hanging around nightclub bars makes you that). I chatted to the chain-smoking Dominic who told me that he was a primary school teacher, so we shared amusing educational anecdotes (and who wouldn't have wanted to be part of that conversation). I also learnt that Roger had worked on the Swiss stock exchange and made a couple of million dollars by borrowing money to increase his stock options which then quadrupled. Consequently they were staying in five-star hotels but complained that some places in south-east Asia had no atmosphere – not surprising really if you live in hotels. The best seats in the house aren't always the best place to experience the show.

We were adopted by a small Indonesian girl, aged around twenty, who firstly latched herself onto Mike in order to tell him that she must sleep with him tonight. In return Mike decided to make conversation by using his Indonesian chat-up line which was something like '*mucha muchante*' – 'you have beautiful eyes'. He was a big fan of Indonesian women but in reality had no interest in someone who just about came up to his waist. Quickly tiring of her protestations of undying love, he tried to ignore her, leading her to try her charms on each one of us in turn with equal success.

It was a long time after when I found out that he actually should have said something closer to '*mata mencintai*'. Quite what she heard, therefore, is anybody's guess, but possibilities include:

Malam mencintai – I love the night
Mas mencintai – I love your gold
Manajer mencintai – I love your manager
Mandi mencintai – I love your bath
Makan mencintai – I love to eat
Mata mahal – Your eyes are expensive
Mata mendidih – I'd like to boil your eyes
Mata mati – Your eyes are dead like an animal
Mati mandi – There's a dead animal in the bath

We decided to check out the dance floor as we couldn't see it from two metres away. It was full of lads who didn't have girlfriends and who seemed to be aspiring to be in some kind of boy band dance competition; we decided it was probably time to call it a night. I suggested to Mike that we meet at 9am as I would be up with all good muslims at 4:30. He said 10am would suit his particular brand of religion (idle agnosticism) more appropriately and we agreed to go to the Kraton – the local Sultan's Palace.

And later that day I was going to find me an erupting volcano.

Lack of Communication
(looking for Merapi)

If you can meet with triumph and disaster
and treat those two imposters just the same

I lay awake until 4am and then waited for the muezzin's call to prayer. Next thing I knew there was a knock at the door – it was Mike and it was 11am; so much for breakfast then. I made my apologies and agreed to meet him in twenty minutes. Quick shower and breakfast and we were wandering in the midday heat down to the Kraton. What's more I'd finally had a decent sleep and felt pretty good.

We walked down Jalan Malioboro (Indonesians are very effective in their use of language – the word for road is *jalan* and the word for walking is *jalan jalan*) and arrived at the main square where we were told by a smartly-dressed man in his 40s that "Palace closed today" but he could show us some really good batik. This brought back memories of the times I had been to Wat Po, the large temple complex in Bangkok, where there would always be an official-looking 'tourist-guide' who would be terribly sorry that the temple was closed today but perhaps he could interest sir in a special jewellery sale. We decided that Wat Po would be an excellent name for a detective-type character – something south-east Asian with the personality of Robbie Coltrane. Ignoring the advice on the palace, we continued on our way with lots of "My name is Po. Wat Po". It seems that every Scottish person in the world can do a half-decent Sean Connery and Mike was able to use his particular skill in a story, which he swore was true, involving his father, Jackie Stewart the racing driver, Sean Connery, a taxi driver and 1960s London.

His father was working for a multinational company and had been tasked with the job of transporting Mr Stewart and Mr Connery from their hotel to a major corporate event – they were running late. There were two taxis waiting outside, one was full with guests on their way to the same function so Mike's dad, Mr Stewart and Mr Connery got into the back of the other. The first taxi sped off and Mike's dad spoke with a sense of urgency to the taxi driver, who was engrossed in his newspaper.

"Follow that car, as quick as you can."

To which the taxi driver, without looking up, replied curtly.

"Alright mate, I ain't bleedin' Jackie Stewart and you ain't James Bond."

There was a brief moment of silence and then a figure leant forward.

"No, but I'm Jackie Stewart."

And after a pause, a quiet voice from the back.

"Yesh... and I'm Jamesh Bond..."

The palace was, of course, open. We paid the fee and the small charge for using a camera and were given a guide for free. He explained in infinite detail the thinking behind every aspect of the palace, e.g. the pillars representing each religion in Java through five different colours – Hindu, Muslim, Buddhist, Catholic and Protestant. The palace complex was very large encompassing areas for bodyguards, harems, armoury, etc. The sultan obviously had a large amount of respect around here, stemming from both the long family history and the ability to retain a certain amount of independence from the various threats made to his people's way of life – this included the Dutch, the Japanese and even Suharto when he was at the height of his powers. There were models displaying the various outfits that were worn for ceremonial occasions and an area, which I think was used for speeches, that echoed really loudly when you clapped. Our guide told us of visits by 'Illary Clinton' and 'Lady Dee' and asked us to take good reports of Jogya with us back to England – we assured him we would.

I had a lot to do that afternoon so Mike and I agreed to meet at 9pm. I had to get some money changed and so went down to the BNI bank. On the way I was hailed by one of the andong drivers – the small horse-drawn carriages that went up and down Jalan Malioboro. He only wanted something ridiculous like 20p to take me there and back so I hopped on and regally trotted down to the bank, market stalls sweeping by on one side, the clamour of traffic on the other. The bank had good rates, 20% better than the airport. I was approached by a young Indonesian who wanted to buy dollars – I would have been quite happy to sell but I had travellers cheques so I apologised. I changed £40 and $100 and was shocked at the wad of notes I received – 2,000,000Rp in 20,000 and 50,000Rp notes. I split them into two piles and shoved one down my sock. Outside my driver was waiting and we clopped with the occasional clip up to the mall where I picked up my cheap glasses. I walked back to the guest house to prepare for my trip to the erupting Merapi volcano; I'd decided that 60,000Rp for the late night trip was too much. It's strange how travelling skews your view of money – £3 would normally be a bargain but when you're talking about 50p a night for accommodation it totally changes your perceptions. I also enjoyed the challenge of trying to get somewhere under my own steam, there's always a danger when backpacking that you end up only staying in backpacker places, taking backpacker excursions and avoiding direct contact with the country you're in as much as possible; do it yourself and you never know quite what you might encounter. And like Captain Scarlet, I'm indestructible, so clearly nothing bad can happen.

The plan was to get a public bus at around 3pm, stay up there for sunset, watch the lava in the dark and get back at around 8pm. I stopped at a café for lunch and chatted to the waiter about this. He said I couldn't get a bus to Kaliang (the nearest village) but there was a good trip for 60,000Rp. This can be the frustrating thing about travelling; ask a simple question and you usually get the answer that will provide the most benefit to the person you asked. Of course, sometimes you may get a genuine answer but it's very difficult to tell the difference. I decided his next statement was going to be "I have friend who…" and so told him I was aware of the trip but was going tomorrow and so couldn't do it.

"Maybe you could get bus but last one back at five-thirty," he advised.

Was that true or was he just trying to put me off? I decided to take it with a pinch of salt, bade him farewell and marched off to the bus sub-terminal. It was a hot and hazy afternoon and the streets were quiet. I walked about three kilometres from the centre and just as I was beginning to doubt my navigation skills I spotted a collection of dodgy looking bemos parked on a muddy lot – bemos are the minivans with bench seats that are the main sort of public transportation in most Indonesian towns; imagine a bus the size of a Ford Fiesta.

I asked which one would take me to Kaliang and a man pointed to a small brown 'twelve-seater' just pulling off. I ran after it shouting.

"Kaliang? Berapa?"

The driver told me 2,000Rp and as I clambered in the side I found myself facing the oldest woman in the world, who beckoned me to sit down and started chatting. I smiled and nodded in the right places and understood nothing – I wish I'd made an effort to learn the language. The guy hanging out of the door barked at the driver and we stopped to pick up passengers; the old woman and I began to get very cosy as she rested her toothless head against my shoulder – I know I hadn't pulled yet this holiday but this was ridiculous. The stopping became annoyingly regular. Women with shopping, lads with cigarettes and young muslim girls, their heads covered by crisp white headscarves. The old woman engaged me in conversation once more and then chuckled a few comments at her fellow passengers which I took to be something along the lines of "Oooh, what a nice young man – if I was eighty years younger…". Everybody giggled.

Suburban Jogya flew by precariously and the small amount of breeze squeezing into the hot interior was very welcome. Another stop and a small boy aged seven or eight, smartly dressed in his school uniform of black shorts and short-sleeved white shirt, climbed on and sat quietly, deep in his own seven or eight year old thoughts. There were now seventeen people on the 'bus', plus the driver and conductor who was now attached to the rest of us by just four fingers, an opposable thumb and a flip-flop. The bus stopped for another three lads. They squatted and bent and hung on to anything that came to hand and off we went. One stop later and the passenger count started getting a bit more sensible. A man in a wheelchair was helped off at the next stop (the wheelchair was on the roof) without the fuss that I had once seen on a bus in England. He was followed by the schoolboy who marched purposefully off home.

Suburbia turned into light jungle punctuated by the occasional house and gradually the bemo emptied until I was the last remaining. The driver beckoned me off.

"Here?" I asked.

He nodded.

I disembarked. A village, of sorts, stretched up and down the road; a long collection of concrete buildings and wooden shacks, several possessing the creamy-whitish-grey satellite dishes that are ever-present in even the smallest outposts of south-east Asia. And of a size that would enable a Bond villain or any enemy of capitalist imperialism to track and bring down Western fighter aircraft with the minimum of effort.

I looked around for a sign saying 'volcano this way', didn't find it, and so began to trudge uphill; it seemed to make sense to go that way. Ten minutes later I reached what seemed to pass as a police station. The officer was lying on a couch watching TV (or maybe attempting to bring down Western fighter aircraft).

"Permisi," I said. He rose, tightening his belt around an unruly stomach and adjusting his gun. "How far Kaliang? Merapi?"

He looked confused.

I pointed to my watch and did a walking impression.

"Merapi? Kaliang? How far?"

He showed me seven fingers which I chose to assume meant minutes. I thanked him and set off. He returned to his work.

Ten minutes later and I couldn't see anything either resembling a volcano or looking like a sign for a volcano. Two teenage girls were standing by the roadside. I walked over to them.

"Permisi. Berapa Kaliang?"

They looked confused.

"I want Merapi. Kaliang. How far?" I asked, pointing at my watch and doing my excellent walking impression again.

"Kaliang," stated one of them. "Ohhhhh."

She pointed to a milepost on the other side of the road which said 'Klang 17 KM'. I looked at it for a moment as slowly everything came clear. I was nowhere near the place. No wonder the policeman was confused (though god knows what the seven finger direction represented); and as for the bastard bus driver who took my money and then dropped me off when he'd had enough.

But you have to laugh, as did the two girls at stupid-Englishman-in-middle-of-nowhere.

It seemed a good idea to ask them when the next bus was but they didn't understand.

I tried asking them why they were waiting here and were they going to Kaliang. They didn't understand.

I felt very stupid for not knowing the language.

I pointed to my watch and tried to do an impression of a bus (big rectangular arm movements, driving impression, 'brum-brum-brum' noises).

"Ohhhhh. Small car," replied one of them.

I nodded my head intently only afterwards thinking what an absurd description of a bus this was; though given the size of them in this neck of the woods it was actually quite an accurate description. They pointed to my watch indicating twenty minutes – around 4:30.

"Small car, Kaliang to Jogya?" I asked. They indicated 5:30.

Bollocks, even if I got there I couldn't get back. I stood there in thought for a while and had an intermittent conversation involving "What your name?" and "Where you from?" One of the girls wandered off and then a small lad on a motorbike joined us.

"Hello," I said.

"Hello," said he. "Where you from?"

"England"

"Oh. Where you going?"

"I want to go to Kaliang to see Merapi but no bus," I explained, with some sense of relief that he was better at foreign languages than I was.

"No," he said, helpfully.

He thought a while.

"Maybe I take you."

I wondered what the catch was.

"What? You take me to Merapi?"

"Yes. We talk English… no money," he added.

"Bloody hell," I thought. Get to Merapi, watch for around a half hour and get the last bus back.

"Okay."

And we were off.

He introduced himself as Ecu (or Ecu 2 as I mentally referred to him), aged 23 (but looking 14) and a student. He wanted to practise his English as he hoped to get a job in a hotel in Jogya. We chatted about his mother (housewife) and father (businessman), education (he worked really hard) and the military (he wasn't sure about military service) as we slowly wound our way up the steep hills. His motorbike seemed slightly overwhelmed at the two of us using its services but struggled on nonetheless, adopting the tone of a household drill slowly going through concrete or a large fly with some very heavy shopping.

Eventually we arrived at a viewing area overlooking a scene of deep ravines and limestone cliffs covered in vegetation. Unfortunately, it was very cloudy and my mountain of fire, apparently in the distance, was not to be seen. I asked if it was possible to get to the scientific base on the volcano, which was apparently an excellent observation spot, but Ecu said it would take too long – so much for seeing the exploding Merapi. I should have been disappointed at this but by now I was actually grateful that I'd got this far.

I found out later that Merapi was one of the most active volcanoes in Indonesia and regular eruptions resulted in pyroclastic flows (fast-moving avalanches of hot ash and rock) and lahars (mud slides) that from time to time devastated the surrounding countryside, often causing fatalities. It had even made the list of the top ten deadliest eruptions of the twentieth century when in 1930 it killed 1,369 people. Perhaps these are the kind of things I should research in advance.

We chatted about life around here and he told me about village children on the other side of the deep ravine who had to traverse this area every day in order to get to the road to get the bus to school – pretty impressive commitment, I thought.

"Come," he said.

I thought it was time to go but he then drove me up to a village of guest houses and cafés set in volcanic cliffs that was obviously the end of the line. I offered to buy him a coke but he refused so I had one myself. We chatted about his religion and the fact he was a strict Muslim and had to pray five times each day. He asked me if I liked beer and said he never drank it but he was interested in life in England and what it was like with alcohol – mostly fine, I said, but with some real idiots who reacted badly to it. He grinned, seemingly unable to see the attraction of such an insidious product.

He then informed me that he would be happy to take me all the way back to Jogya. Was I grateful! He asked if it would be okay if we stopped in his village on the way which I said was fine. We set off down the steep, winding road and were soon being chased by a frenetically beeping scooter. It was two of Ecu's friends, obviously curious.

"Where you from?" they shouted as we sped frantically around a corner.

"England," I replied.

"Ahh, David Bekkem, Lady Dee," they shouted.

"Manchester United," I replied, pointing at myself. "You?"

"Yes," they yelled.

They chatted away to Ecu as they weaved their way towards a small village. We turned up a side road and the lads accelerated after a chicken that ran in a panic and then flung itself indignantly into a bush.

"Very bad," I shouted, smiling.

"Bad boy," they replied with broad grins.

We negotiated potholes to Ecu's house and stopped. He pointed to the door.

"Please go in."

I pointed to my boots, remembering Javanese decorum.

"Should I take these off?"

"No. No problem."

I went in and sat down.

Ecu brought a large calendar over. I had told him that I was likely to return to Jogya and he wanted to know when so that we could meet up. Panic – I'd have to make some definite plans! I counted back from the 23rd when I was flying and said I would probably be here on the 19th or 20th. Ecu said he couldn't make the 19th because of school but if we met on the 20th he could take me anywhere I wanted to go. I thanked him for his kindness and gave him my home address so he could write if he wished. We got up to leave and I briefly met his mother, smiling and graceful in a long golden sarong, whose hand I shook with a smile and a nod. I bid farewell to the lads and we started the longish journey to Jogya.

As we sped along the thankfully quiet roads, he asked me about my girlfriend, which I made up as it was bad form in Indonesia not to have one; especially as I told him I was 30 and he'd told me that Indonesian Muslims should be married by then. I didn't know what label I would have been given had I said I was single but I guessed it could have been freak, gay or communist; whichever way I didn't want to risk having to walk. Ecu had a girlfriend whom he saw on Fridays and intended to marry if he got the hotel job he wanted. He asked me about life in England ranging from the royal family to the welfare state. I explained as best I could and said maybe he'd visit one day. He said it was unlikely and I guessed it probably was. His pay would be between £2 and £5 per week for the next few years. It made me appreciate more the opportunities in England and once again question those people who moaned about their standard of living in one of the richest countries in the world.

He tentatively asked me if I'd give him some money so that he could put some petrol in his motorbike and we stopped at the organised chaos of the local petrol station. To be fair, the forecourt itself was much the same as in the UK; it was the seemingly random queuing system that I couldn't understand. We joined a scrum of motorbikes and blokes filling petrol cans (which looked suspiciously like five litre orange squash bottles) who were being tended by two attendants, one with the cash and one who was able to fill up everything in sight without stopping his flow of petrol; I could tell that in his nonchalant way he was very proud of this skill. We managed to fill our tank without any major spillage and I was pleased that we didn't have to wait too closely to the two guys smoking cigarettes under the large '*Dilarang merokok*' ('No smoking') sign. Ten minutes later we were battling through the cloudy, noisy approaches to Jalan Malioboro.

Ecu dropped me at the entrance to Jalan Sosro and said he'd try to find me here on the 20th. The other Ecu hailed me over to sort out my ticket to Mount Bromo and on to Bali. The smouldering Bromo had been strongly recommended and the price of 100,000Rp for an 'executive' coach, Band B, sunrise at the volcano and on to Bali seemed excellent – even if it did start at 7am the next day.

We then went to see the guitar man as I thought that a £20 personalised guitar was too good to miss. I had a long chat with him (via Ecu) explaining exactly what I wanted – acoustic pick-ups, dark green, and my initials; we agreed a price of 375,000Rp. I gave him 100,000Rp deposit saying I wanted it to be the best guitar he'd ever made and I would collect it on the 20th.

I returned to the guest house, changed and set off to catch Mike early as he said he may be on the internet. He wasn't so I grabbed a coffee at Superman II. Indonesian coffee – outstanding. Ground coffee is put straight into a cup, hot water poured onto it and as much sugar as you like; get to the bottom and the sludge is like an environmental calamity. An even bigger treat meets those who like it white – condensed milk. Don't stir it and it's like drinking a black and white lava lamp; give it a stir and it's a cross between molten steel and Baileys. Fantastic. You'd have to staple your eyes to keep them shut.

Happily fixed I went for another wander and spotted Mike in a café with a few other backpackers dotted around. He asked me what

I'd been up to today – it took me a good ten minutes to give him the brief version. He shot off to get changed and I started to chat to a Dutch girl sitting at the table opposite. She told me she was from Rotterdam but I didn't hear her properly and so said I hadn't heard of it which made me sound really stupid. Her boyfriend came back from wherever he'd been and we ordered food. Mike then returned and we made small talk about football, etc. We got on to languages and as I was commenting on how good the Dutch were, an Indonesian sat down with us and started chatting in English and then Dutch. He then went on to use his French, German, Spanish and a little bit of Italian – we were impressed. Mike, however, inexplicably knew a Zimbabwean dialect which no-one could really beat.

Later that evening Mike and I returned to the Borobudur bar that seemed to have the same band and definitely the same Madonna video. We decided not to have a repeat experience with the Guinness. I started slagging off their musical prowess and Mike quickly wandered off due to what I assumed were artistic differences. The next thing I knew the band were calling *Neek* to the stage for a karaoke version of 'New York, New York'. I hid under the table in a pathetic pretence of sorting out my shoelaces but as the calls for *Neek* became louder I poked my head up in a look of mock surprise. However, before I could move, an inflated Chinese gentlemen had made his way to the stage as the first few bars of the song began to ring out. A sea of swaying Indonesians faced him as big white letters shouted out from the screen previously inhabited by Madonna singing 'Like a Virgin'.

"Start spreading the news," he appeared to mime. Someone, it seemed, had turned off the microphone.

He attempted to fiddle with the on/off switch on the mike as the words "I'm leaving today" flickered by. A burst of feedback screamed through the room and he launched into the song.

"Thees fagabond shoooss…" he yelled tunelessly.

"Are longing to stayeee … "

And gaining in confidence he began to prowl the stage like a large not-very-good-at-prowling thing.

By now Mike had returned to our table and the band were glaring at us as if we were completely responsible. We shrugged our shoulders as the Frank Sinatra tribute turned from comedy into farce. A misjudged high kick unbalanced the King of Swing and as his hand pleaded for moral support from the microphone stand he tumbled backwards into the drum kit. It must be very rare in life that a comic fall is genuinely accompanied by the noise of a tom-tom, snare and cymbal.

As the letters on the big screen claimed he was 'King of the Hill' and 'Top of the List', the deflated Chinese gentlemen extricated himself from a hi-hat and limped his way back to his business colleagues as Mike and I wiped the tears from our eyes. The rest of the evening passed by in a more uneventful way as the band re-assembled the drum kit and went into a surprisingly good version of 'Linger' by The Cranberries followed by a car-crash attempt at 'Hound Dog'. A random girl came over, asked Mike a question, laughed, and then did the same to another table.

"What did she want?" I asked.

"She wanted to know if we were Americans."

Mortally offended by this I called her over and asked her to explain herself. Apparently she had been playing 'guess the nationality' with some friends; I had a baseball cap on so I guess I was asking for it. We chatted to her for a while and Mike went into sharking mode but denied it later. By about 11:00 I was getting tired and as we had to be up for 7:00 the next day I went back to the hotel and packed.

I flicked off the lights and lay underneath the fan with a smile. My journey was finally taking on its own personality; I quite liked it.

Fulfilment of Dreams
(discovering volcanoes)

Rosy-fingered morning came forth
from the first grey dawn

Say what you like about the Germans but they're very good at doing indignant.

I got to the departure point on Jalan Sosro at the required time but with that time looking increasingly flexible I grabbed some strange looking curried egg and rice for breakfast from an old woman sitting on the pavement with a pile of curried eggs and a pile of rice resting on yesterday's newspapers. Mike turned up and we were led onto the bus – the kind of battered old bus they used in towns with no leg room, luggage space or air-con; and we had a fifteen hour journey to Bromo. As we acquired passengers from around the town the mood got darker and darker as we all contemplated a lifetime inside this sorry vehicle. Most of us, especially those of British extraction, grumped quietly but said nothing. However, at the final stop before the journey a mid-30s German guy decided that the group of Indonesians standing by the door clearly had some kind of responsibility for this miserable attempt at luxury travel and enough was enough. His outraged rant, as well as being entertaining, was also enough for all of us to get off the bus in a show of solidarity. It was only two minutes before our executive air-conditioned 'luxury' bus appeared and we all rushed on with the aim that transcends all cultures – the quest for a double seat each. Success.

The bus set off and I watched the co-driver with a worried expression as he occasionally peered out of the side window to check if the luggage doors were closed properly and the wheels were still on. I caught up on my diary and tried to sleep. At other times I amused myself by watching overtaking manoeuvres. The roads in Indonesia are incredible – becaks, motorcycles, cars, buses, lorries and chickens, all clamouring for space. A single piece of road can vary in width several times over a mile and the edge is marked by white paint on trees, rocks or anything else you may want to miss.

I wondered if they had a written driving test and what it may include:

When is it appropriate to overtake?
a) When the road is clear and it is safe to do so.
b) When you are bigger than the oncoming traffic.

When overtaking should you:
a) Show courtesy to other drivers and not cause them to swerve or slow down.
b) Beep your horn furiously.

If involved in an accident with a larger vehicle on your side of the road, is it:
a) Their fault for being on the wrong side of the road.
b) Your fault because you're smaller.

We bumped and swerved along roads lined with paddy fields and palm trees. Villages came and went; each with its standard issue of mangy dog, family of chickens, lad sitting idly on motorbike, and small child sitting cross-legged by roadside playing with broken plastic toy. From time to time we were treated to a cow, a washed-out bridge or a group of lads attempting to sell cigarettes and crisps at junctions. Occasionally we winced as our driver clipped the mirrors of oncoming trucks.

After another short kip, I looked opposite and saw a huge dark reflection. For a moment I couldn't work out what it was but then realised that the large dark thing was outside and was a monstrous volcano. Mike looked at my shock.

"You should have seen the one behind it."

This is what I came for.

At the next stop I excitedly jumped out of the coach to take a picture. Unfortunately we were in a petrol station and I'd forgotten to put my shoes on – this didn't do my white sports socks much good, but then I guess that served me right for possessing and wearing white socks.

As the sun went down behind us, a small group congregated at the back of the bus to take a picture of the sunset and wave at confused but vaguely amused Indonesians.

It was dark when we stopped but I think we had reached Probolinggo and we changed to a smaller bus for the final ascent to Bromo. Mike and I sat at the front with an air of anticipation as the winding road took us steadily upwards. My anticipation manifested itself as a quiet contemplation of what I might see. Mike's on the other hand involved him talking incessantly. These were slightly at odds. We arrived at our hotel in what I guessed was Ngadisari, at about 9pm. Our rooms were all on the second floor and had spectacular views of volcanic cliffs. A blonde girl in her early 20s walked past me to the room next door.

"Pretty impressive, isn't it?" I said by way of a greeting.

She agreed. Her name was Anna and she came from Wimborne in Dorset, an area I knew well from holidays in the New Forest. Mike came over so I introduced him and we all decided to have dinner together. She explained she was on a round-the-world trip taking in Fiji and Australia amongst others – she would soon be off to Malaysia and Thailand and then back to England to continue her training as a doctor. Over a very mediocre meal of uninspiring satay and a small plastic plate of cold rice we chatted about travelling and shared stories. Afterwards we went out to admire the clear night. It was cool and fresh outside and the stars were as crisp as I'd ever seen them. We wandered into another guest house where a sour-faced Dutch guy hijacked us and told us how the only way to see the volcano properly was by hiring a Jeep otherwise we'd have to walk 10 kilometres. It's difficult to know who and what to believe when travelling and we didn't really give him much credence, mainly because he was sour-faced, but we booked the Jeep anyway because we thought it would be fun and it was only 17,500Rp each. By now it was 11:30 so we retired to our rooms and I crept under my blankets ready for a 3am start.

Half an hour later there was a knock at the door – it was 3am. I grunted and lay in shock for twenty minutes. Jeeps were waiting outside and we left at 3:30. Sitting with the three of us were a cheerful Aussie couple who were a little bit too enthusiastic for that time of day, so I sat quietly in the front. We stopped in Semeru Lawang for some hot drinks; some people said they'd rather have had a lie in but I was glad of the hot chocolate. We got back in the Jeeps and started the long journey to the viewpoint.

I had no idea where we were going and little idea of what to expect. The Tengger caldera, which contained the flattened cones of Bromo and several others, was a 10 kilometre wide crater that had been formed by the eruption of a bigger volcano millions of years ago. As we descended onto the ancient caldera's volcanic plain I looked into the blackness hoping to catch my first sight of what it was like to be in a crater of this size; the lights of the Jeep revealed nothing but lava sand. We sped across the relatively smooth surface and commented on how much fun this would be on motorbikes. A sharp right and we started a climb varying between 1:4 to 1:3 with tight curves ever upwards. 5am and we were still climbing. We reached a log jam of Jeeps at around 5:30, disembarked and were pointed up a steep track. I had rather naively expected a sparsely-populated mountain-top but instead it was packed full of people of all nationalities. Anna, Mike and I found a prime spot where I was able to rest my camera on a wall in order to get a long exposure time in the low light. A fierce wind was hitting us from the east and cutting through the poorly chosen clothes I was wearing – I hadn't planned for it to be this cold at an altitude of nearly 3,000 metres.

The sky began to lighten with the first appearance of the rosy fingers of dawn and we were able to make sense of our position: towards the sun were the deep valleys we had come through to reach the hotel and still hidden by fading night was the volcanic plain containing Bromo, Batok, Kursi, and the massive Mount Semeru in the distance. Clouds lay low below us but we could see glimpses of various features and it added to the mystical quality of the place. I felt increasingly cold but continued to take photos as the light changed; unfortunately my camera decided to complain about the temperature by switching off the light meter and leaving the shutter open. This induced major panic and forgetting about the beginnings of mild hypothermia I shoved the frozen metal box up my sweatshirt. The sun eventually appeared, later than expected and not the clear sunrise we desired. But it was a special moment nevertheless with glimpses through the clouds of volcanic cliffs and deep fertile valleys – if this wasn't the top of the world, it wasn't far off.

There seemed to be a slight sense of anti-climax amongst some of the gathering as they moved to look at the volcanic plain behind us. Unfortunately the slight increase in air temperature had caused a mass of cloud and there was virtually nothing to see apart from the distant peak of Mount Semeru. The crowd was reduced to perhaps a dozen who were still enchanted with the place. I was waylaid by the sour-faced Dutch guy who muttered something about "Oh wasn't so good." I could see Mike and Anna scurrying away chuckling as I mushed his head into a pulp and posted it to his parents – sorry, smiled and nodded politely.

By 6:30 it was still extremely cloudy but we were sure it would improve and as we waited there seemed to be a noticeable clearing of the clouds. Gradually we could see the sun reaching the valley below us and as the wind continued, the smoking Bromo came into view. We all pulled our cameras out in unison with gasps of awe. The clouds moved in again but when they cleared once more we couldn't believe our eyes. Mount Semeru in the distance had let forth a massive plume of dark smoke and ash – this was a volcano doing its business right in front of us! We gasped and laughed and then ran around in circles with excitement. There was hardly anybody left to witness this but here we were. We watched for another twenty minutes as the dark grey cloud slowly dispersed but as the clouds gathered again we began to wonder whether our Jeep would still be there. We decided that the nice Aussies wouldn't let it go without us but we shouldn't keep them waiting much longer so we made our way back down.

They were there with the driver so we got on board and set off. Halfway down we looked to our left and witnessed the most incredible sight – the clouds had cleared to reveal the sweeping browns, greys and greens of the massive caldera with the perfect flattened cones of Bromo and Batok sitting directly below us on the volcanic plain. The whole Jeep shouted 'Stop!' in unison.

"Stop here?" The driver replied with a nonchalant smile and as the Jeep rolled to halt we bounded out and gasped in wonderment – this was the real thing. We imagined dinosaurs prowling, Mongol raiders on horseback, Martian landings. And there was Bromo smoking away. It was difficult to get a sense of perspective of this vast area until I spotted the distant temple nestling bravely at the foot of the volcanoes. I took a touristy shot of Anna grinning inanely and Mike took the same of me, leaning on a railing with the golden-brown scene behind me. I got back into the Jeep gushing – this was the best place I had ever seen and I couldn't remember being so excited. We tried to compare Niagara Falls – over-rated, the Grand Canyon – pretty good, and Victoria Falls – Mike said they were impressive; but this was just so different, so breathtaking – it certainly seized my imagination.

We continued our descent and once onto the plain we sped across the sea of sand towards the smoking grey cone of Bromo. Its most recent notable eruption had been in October 1995 when a column of ash had risen 700 metres above the rim, causing ashfall 20 kilometres away, but it was looking slightly calmer today. As we approached, we could see the congregation of Jeeps and tourists and nearby was the Hindu temple looking surprisingly larger than it had first appeared.

There was a large collection of locals with small horses offering horseback rides halfway up the steep climb – the rest, rather disappointingly, was concrete steps (I was hoping for a death-defying scramble), but still steep and still impressive. I set off quickly but then thought it might be polite to wait for everyone else. After five seconds I was bored of politeness and thought it would be fun to ride a horse for the advertised price of 1,000Rp. I wasn't an equestrian expert but I was sure my feet weren't supposed to touch the ground as I placed my backside in the saddle. With a little bit of encouragement my boots squeezed into the narrow stirrups and, guided by the owner, my little pony panted and stumbled over the rocks up to the concrete steps which led to the top.

I was nodded in the direction of the summit and marched purposefully upwards. A third of the way up and my marching turned to slow, steady steps with the odd rest to take photographs of the now beautifully sunlit caldera. As I reached the top I was breathing deeply – that was when the sulphur hit me hard. I tried to turn away and breathe through my sweatshirt but with limited success. The pungent smell of rotten eggs wrapped around me like an old blanket and I felt my body silently struggling for oxygen as the smoke drifted through me. Thankfully the wind changed and as I reached the 2,400 metre crater edge I was able to breath clearer air. I looked inside the 700 metre diameter crater, half expecting bubbling lava but knowing that most volcanoes weren't really like that at all. The steep grey cliffs descended to an uneven surface with fissures pushing out great clouds of sulphur, the wind gusting it over the narrow rim to my left; behind me was the wide sandsea plain and the fertile Mount Batok. Here I was, an ambition achieved.

Mike and Anna joined me and we wandered along the narrow rim. I took a photo of a small figure making the long and dangerous journey all the way round the cone; had we the time I would have done the same. As it was we took some precarious looking shots teetering on the edge and admired the view. Mike trekked down relatively quickly due to the sulphur but Anna and I stayed a little longer with the handful of people looking around in wonder. Sadly, it was approaching 8:00 and time to get back for breakfast and the 9:00 bus to Bali. We quickly descended and on finishing the steps I abandoned Anna and jumped on my steed. She laughed and said she had to take a photo so I handed her my camera and sat, allegedly looking ridiculous – I thought I was Lawrence of Indonesia. Desperately leaning back and trying to use the narrow stirrups, I took the track downwards; as a final flourish I cantered to the Jeeps and with what I regarded as great finesse came to a reasonably controlled halt. This could have been quite impressive but as I jumped off my trusty friend my left foot stayed firmly fixed inside its stirrup and with a dull thump I landed on my back with one leg in the air. I picked myself up in a feeble attempt to look like it was all planned and strutted to the Jeep. Mr Aussie grinned and introduced himself as Gary and his wife as Bev – it was now a slightly more reasonable time for conversation. They'd apparently done the horse thing as well and felt as ridiculous as I probably looked. Gary and Bev were pretty much what your average British person imagines your average Aussie to be like – cheerful, open-minded and good company – a bit of a stereotype but not a bad one to be.

Back at the hotel, we cheerfully breakfasted together, but my mind constantly wandered back to Bromo. Mike was intending to stay a couple of days and was probably going to hire a motorbike, go back to the viewpoint and take some pictures while it was clear. This sounded like a great idea and gave me the thought of staying, doing the same and the two of us hiring horses and doing some serious riding across the wide flat plain. The whole plan sounded brilliant so I asked the hotel if I could get the next day's bus and was given the all clear. Mike and I shook hands with glee and I imagined leading the Arab revolt across the desert and storming a heavily-defended city. The timing of my trip would be messed up a little but it seemed worth it. We said a hearty goodbye to Gary and Bev while Anna shot upstairs to pack her stuff. I followed her up, did the e-mail-address-swapping thing and made a tentative arrangement to meet up in Kuta with Mike as well. Everybody safely on the bus, Mike and I discussed a plan – move hotels, sleep for two hours, hit the crater. We went to our rooms to pack. Suddenly there was a call from downstairs.

"Number twelve. Number twelve." I looked at my door – it was me. "You get bus now."

"Er, no. I speak to two people they say I go tomorrow. No problem."

"Yes problem. Tomorrow small bus full. No have room, you no get on."

Crestfallen, I looked at Mike. I thought it would probably be okay tomorrow but I couldn't take the risk of being here for three days if it wasn't. I'd have to go.

I quickly threw my belongings together and made arrangements to e-mail Mike and hopefully meet in Kuta on the 9th. As I jumped on the bus, Anna, Gary and Bev looked up with a quizzical look. I briefly explained the situation and plonked myself down next to Anna. I was gutted, I'd been torn between staying and going but once Mike and I had chatted about our plans I had psyched myself up for fun in this incredible setting.

I chatted to Anna as we made our way down but all I really wanted to do was stop the bus and jump off.

Continuing East
(off to Bali)

A good traveller has no fixed plans

We changed onto the decent air-con bus and spread ourselves out again. I was feeling pretty tired and unsociable. We stopped for lunch but I was too tired to eat; I forced some food down and chatted to the genial Gary about his cleaning company with my mind elsewhere. The journey continued in a blur of green and eventually we reached the coast and ferry to Bali.

Turning down offers of water, pineapple, crisps and rice, we found a spot on the covered deck and were quickly surrounded by kids, most of whom wanted us to pay them money to make massive leaps from the ferry roof into the water below. I kept a close eye on my bags and the kids did their jumping. As the ferry left, we could see them swimming around in the docks.

The journey was only around half an hour but we then spent twenty minutes waiting to dock; 'like clockwork' is not an Indonesian phrase; 'rubber time' is. Gary passed the time chatting to some locals and came back saying that a doctor had kindly offered him and Bev a place to stay. Unfortunately they had to go straight to Kuta and get their flight so it wasn't convenient but they were touched by their first experience of Balinese hospitality.

Disembarked at Bali, buses were waiting to take us to our destinations. Anna got on the northern bound Lovina bus as she wanted to see the dolphins and we arranged to meet in the more central town of Ubud the next day. I had decided to go to Ubud as it seemed to be the shortest journey and I was sick of buses; Gary and Bev were on same one as it also went to Kuta. I sat next to the doctor and Gary introduced me. Apparently she lived in Bali but made this journey every day to her practice on Java – maybe four hours there and the same back. She smiled as I told her this was very hard work and replied that it was okay because Saturdays and Sundays were holidays.

We all chatted and the bus rumbled on and on and on. Looking at a map I had naively thought that the journey would be about one hour but it was starting to look like more than three. The doctor left us and I stretched out on the small plastic seats as best I could. Gary and I passed the time discussing the merits or otherwise of luminaries such as Princess Diana, Tony Blair and the woman whose baby was kidnapped by a dingo. We eventually reached Ubud. I again said farewell to my antipodean companions and promised to get their address off Mike. It was 8:30pm.

Herds of young Balinese jumped on me.

"Room?"

"You need room?"

"Where you stay?"

I struggled to get hold of my backpack.

"I'm okay, thank you."

I had carefully studied my Lonely Planet book and knew I wanted to stay at Mandia bungalows where Anna and I had agreed to meet the next day; unfortunately I hadn't studied the map of Ubud properly so didn't know where I was. (Rule number two: Know where you're going.)

"Where you going?"

"Hey, where you going?"

Inquisitive and demanding brown eyes looking at me. I was glad I was tall.

"I'm staying at Mandia. Meeting friend."

They informed me that Mandia was a long way away; I had no idea but assumed they were lying and so said that I knew it wasn't. They then offered me a motorbike lift for 5,000Rp, I said 2,000Rp and started walking so one of them relented and took me for that price. I knew I had probably paid too much but I was shagged.

Mandia was 400 metres down the road. It was full. Next door was full. As were the next three – this was getting silly. Eventually a woman stopped me and showed me a card saying her bungalows were not far and her husband could take me. I asked her how much, she said 30,000Rp and I countered with 20,000Rp. She didn't really agree but I said I'd have a look. I jumped on the back of her husband's motorbike and the trip turned out to be just over a kilometre. We stopped on a quiet looking road and went through into a large garden with a collection of bamboo and brick bungalows. My room was actually quite nice with a hot shower, verandah and free breakfast. I reiterated 20,000Rp and he agreed. Hurrah.

I had a quick shower, got changed and wandered off to find the nearest half-decent restaurant. The first one, the Dirty Duck, was one of the poshest in Ubud – all bamboo mats and water features. It had prices to match – main courses 20-30,000Rp compared to the usual 6,000Rp. I felt I deserved decent food so walked in feeling unkempt and sat at the bar. A waitress brought a menu along and I decided to treat myself to some very nice duck. Fed and watered I wandered back to the guesthouse, sat on the verandah and drank my complimentary tea that sat in a flask by the door.

I was up a volcano this morning.

I awoke at around 11.30 the next day – the first proper night's sleep I'd had since I arrived. I wandered out and was greeted by a friendly chap in a blue and white sarong who obviously ran the place. He brought along a simple breakfast of white toast, honey and papaya within five minutes and I had a leisurely meal. A quick perusal of my map of Ubud and I decided to go for a walk through the Monkey Forest and then out to a few villages.

I was intrigued to see what Bali was really like, as it seemed to have crept its way into popular culture as an exotic island paradise (bigger than the Isle of Wight but smaller than Singapore) with a relaxed and cultured view of life. With its crafts and performing arts, Ubud was regarded as central to this.

In daylight the street was actually quite busy. Up the road I could see small shops selling bamboo wind chimes and kites; down the road were the trees that marked the entrance to the Monkey Forest. I wandered along the pink pavements to the entrance, paid a small amount to enter and took a concrete pathway towards where the action seemed to be. In a central area, shaded by trees, was a collection of monkeys (long-tailed macaques) and an even larger collection of tourists. The monkeys knew that free food was available here and the tourists were very obliging. Handing out bananas and taking photos was the order of the day. Particularly popular was a mother with a small baby hanging underneath and I joined everyone else in an attempt to terrify the infant as much as possible with our black boxes and bright flashes of light.

Realising that this probably wasn't an accurate portrayal of monkeys in their natural habitat I wandered away from all this activity, past two women in aquamarine sarongs who were gracefully sweeping the path and up some steps to the *Pura Dalem* – the Temple of the Dead. This was my first look at a Balinese temple. Balinese religion is based on Hinduism but also has strong elements of animism, which is why the Balinese believe that spirits are everywhere and are constantly laying out offerings to them. The intricate stone temples can vary in size and design but the Temple of the Dead is noted for its strong magical powers and presence of evil spirits. I was greeted by Rangda, the wicked witch-widow with unkempt hair, lolling tongue, gruesome face and large breasts; hobbies, eating children and scaring people.

The temple seemed to be closed so I peered through the gateway at the open-sided pavilions (used for purposes such as storage or artistic performances), the ornate drum tower (announcing temple events and the imminent approach of foes) and the elaborate stone tower, holding the golden door which led into the inner courtyard; this gateway was guarded by fierce Raksa busily stopping evil spirits and helped by Bhoma – who had his hands outstretched either side of his fierce face.

Rangda kindly held a pose while I took her picture and I returned to the forest to investigate some of the tracks leading off the main area. One led down to the river that cut deeply through the forest; the second was smaller and didn't drop as far. At the bottom was a small shrine with stone lizards and various other creatures dappled by sunlight. Retracing my steps, I followed a track through the forest and soon found myself in open countryside. Opposite me, small houses were spread out, many selling woodcarvings and paintings; surrounding them were small paddy fields and forests of palm trees in the distance. After about twenty minutes I was getting hungry so I returned to the forest and walked back onto Monkey Forest Road. It was a steep walk into the main part of town, past small shops selling carvings, jewellery and clothes; past restaurants selling everything from noodles to pancakes; past young guys offering transport; past guesthouses offering cheap rooms. Ubud was attractive, though; not hectic; and clean. It also seemed less troubled by the problems facing the rest of the country. I stopped for food close to the spot where I had arrived the previous day, watched a few barefoot kids kicking a ball around the small football pitch and then made my way back to the bungalows.

The plan was to meet Anna at Mandia that evening at around 8:00 so I chilled out on the quiet verandah for a while, got changed and set off at about 6:00. I stopped at one of the many 'travel agents' (bloke with desk, telephone and large poster of paddy field) on the way in order to find out the cost of getting to Kintamani where I could visit the volcano, Gunung Batur. It was 10,000Rp and buses left twice per day at 9:15 and 12:15. I decided to leave tomorrow on the 9:15 bus – I'd sort out the ticket early in the morning.

I slowly wandered through the town and arrived at Mandia at around 7.30. I checked to see if Anna had arrived and as she hadn't I decided to sit in the attached restaurant, have a long dinner and catch up with my diary. 8:00 came and went as I studied the omnipresent bottles of chilli sauce and tomato sauce that graced the tables of all good Indonesian eateries. These are always accompanied by unhelpfully small, pink paper napkins, two flies and some ants.

By 8:30 I began to think she had been delayed in Lovina – I'd thought that doing it in one day would be good going. I scribbled out a note telling her where I was and my plans for the next few days and decided to deposit it at Mandia in case she arrived later this evening. As I was wandering down the narrow entrance, a young Indonesian spotted me.

"Excuse me sir, can I help you?"

I carefully explained why I was here, for whom I was looking, why she would be coming here and what I wanted, gaining the reply, "But she not stay here."

"Yes, I know, but maybe she arrives today or tomorrow."

"Ahh, but full, she not here."

"Okay, but if she comes can you give her this?"

"She come here?" he said with utter surprise. It was turning into a bad episode of Fawlty Towers.

"Yes, she is coming here to stay, I think tomorrow, can you give her this?" waving the note.

"Oh. Okay. Come this way." He led me to the reception area and handed me a piece of paper. "You want to leave her message?"

"No, can you give her this?"

"She your girlfriend?"

"No, just a friend."

"Okay, I look after it."

"Okay, great. Thank you. Terima kasih. Goodbye."

Mission accomplished – I hoped.

I wandered back to my guest house, past the dark entrance to the Monkey Forest and jumping when a rat sped past me going about his ratty business. On the way I checked out the internet place opposite. It was plush, with decent PCs, and the cost was 7,000Rp (35p) for 15 minutes – I decided to sort it out tomorrow. I returned to the bungalows and wrote my diary for a while but when my hand started to get sore I decided to do the internet thing after all. Unfortunately it was 10:30 and the place was closed – I'd have to do it in the morning. I sat on the verandah and tried to learn some Indonesian for a while. This included "I want to go to…" – "*Saya mau pergi ke*" – and counting, with a failsafe method to remember the numbers:

Satu – one (because it is)

Dua – two (sounds like Spanish or Italian for two)

Tiga – three (imagined Tigger with three tails)

Empat – four (but has five letters)

Lima – five (has four letters, is capital of Peru and Paddington came from there)

Enam – six (…six enamel tiles?)

Tujuh – seven (have a sister called Julia who sometimes acts like she's seven)

Delepan, Sembilan, Sepuluh – eight, nine and ten (have a nice rhythmic feel)

I also learned 'What time is it?' – '*Jam berapa?*', 'Two o'clock.' – '*Jam dua.*','How many hours?' – '*Berapa jam?*', and 'Seven hours.' – '*Tujuh jam.*'

With jams and tigas ringing in my ears, I set the alarm for 7am in order to give me plenty of time to sort out the 9:15 bus to Kintamani and Mount Batur.

Wandering
(still in Ubud)

Selamat siang

I woke up at 8.45 – so much for that plan. The cheerful chap at the bungalows brought me my breakfast and I asked him to sort out a 12:15 ticket for me. He returned after five minutes saying this service didn't happen any more so unless I sorted out an alternative, I'd have to go tomorrow morning. I hadn't found Ubud appealing enough to stay another day – a bit too touristy – but I reasoned it would give me a chance to do some e-mailing, laundry and general wandering. I bought a ticket for the next day and had breakfast. Whilst I was eating he told me about a traditional show that was happening in one of the temples, a performance of the Ramayana in typical Balinese style, big costumes and a traditional gamelan orchestra. I knew a little about gamelan, its complex sounds and rhythms produced from a mix of xylophones, cymbals and drums and I told him I'd speak to him later.

I walked over to the internet place and messaged Mike to say I couldn't meet him in Kuta on the 8th but would meet him on the 18th. I also e-mailed Anna in case she didn't get the message I'd left with Manuel at Mandia.

I decided to wander up the road on which I was staying and began to realise how attractive it was. After dropping off some laundry, I walked past a number of old red-bricked Balinese houses and temples. The locals had been busy offering gifts to the spirits – food in small parcels littered the pavements. It reminded me of the gifts that Thai people leave in the small spirit houses they have on their land.

I stopped off at a pleasant restaurant called Nomads and bought a paper from a young boy. Apart from the economic upheaval, the big story in the English language paper *The Jakarta Post*, was the shock of many of its readers at the treatment of Chinese women during the recent riots and a government member's reactions to this. The Chinese had been targeted by more extreme members of Muslim community due to their alleged corrupt dealings with the government and perceived control over many aspects of Indonesian business. This had resulted in Chinese homes and businesses being ransacked and reports of the rape of Chinese women. A member of the government had poured scorn on many of the claims and had pretty much dismissed it as attention-seeking. Consequently the letters page and the paper's own editorial was incensed by his comments and it seemed clear to me that things must be slowly changing for the better if at least newspapers could criticise government representatives in this way.

I looked down the street at life going on as usual. Bali seemed to be a long way from these events with no visible evidence or reports of this kind of trouble. I was later told by a local that it was bad for business. A pleasantly pragmatic attitude but from what I'd read and seen it seemed that the Balinese were a much more tolerant people than some others in Indonesia.

I continued on to the market – a quiet, two-storey courtyard with scores of stalls selling spices, carvings, masks, material, clothes, all piled as high and as deep as possible. An elderly woman in a blue sarong and gold top smiled as she walked past me and I returned the compliment. I stood and watched an old man skilfully chopping at large, orange papayas with the short machete (or *parang*) that seemed to be the main tool of choice in Indonesia. Wandering in and out of the morning sun and ducking under wooden monkeys and gentle wind chimes, I came across a friendly man selling fake watches – good fakes and the Tag style that I wanted. I made appreciative noises and told him I'd return later. I reached the junction with Monkey Forest Road but instead of turning left I carried straight on, past a CD shop and stopped to buy some traditional Balinese food (an iced bun and some crisps). The road fell between high cliffs and I took a track leading up to some arable land. I was met with a view of palms, paddy fields and a string of people going about their work beneath the warm sky.

I had read that the way in which villagers work together and particularly the organisation of wet-rice paddies is one of the most important elements of Balinese society. It is controlled by a subak – a group of people responsible for the planting, harvesting of paddy fields and, most importantly, the flow of water; any farmer wishing to change the flow of water in or out of a paddy must first agree this with the subak. Interdependency and co-operation are two very important concepts in Balinese society and I guessed it permeated right through all types of Balinese business dealings; this would explain why someone always has a 'friend' who can provide you with the product or service you may or may not need.

I took a couple of pictures and continued down the road. A pair of sunlit bridges crossed a deep ravine where two rivers joined and flowed into the town. One bridge carried traffic whereas the other, obviously older bridge sat beside it looking picturesque. In the river below there were some Balinese women bathing and washing clothes. I crossed the bridge, took some photos and was approached by a couple of guys trying to sell paintings and woodcarvings. They enthusiastically asked all about me in the hope that it would make it more likely that I would buy something but I politely refused and returned to town.

I wandered around the supermarket and CD shops and then walked back through the market – maybe I would buy those watches after all. I found the watch-man.

"Hello my good friend," he said with a smile.

I decided to try to conduct business in Indonesian.

"*Selamat siang* (Good day). *Berapa?*"

I obviously sounded confident enough as he responded in Indonesian; I gathered that the watches I wanted were 80,000Rp each.

"*Tidak, mahal* (No, expensive)," I said gravely.

He thought about this and reduced the price to 60,000Rp. I offered him 30,000Rp (*tiga puluh ribu* – literally 'three ten thousand'), with a smile, and he went into a long speech about what I guessed was the wonderful quality of his merchandise and how he was the most worthy trader this side of Antarctica. I nodded in what I thought were the appropriate places. At this point I told him that I actually wanted two and would give him 80,000Rp for both. He went into another speech and with the help of a calculator came up with the figure 130,000Rp – I'm not quite sure how. After I protested, this was reduced to 120,000Rp.

"Okay, okay," I said. "*Sembilan puluh ribu* (90,000)."

He suggested 110,000.

I then wanted to offer him 100,000 but at this point my language deserted me and instead of saying 100 – *seratus* – I said "*Sepuluh puluh*" – tenty or ten tens – which doesn't mean anything.

He gave me a funny look but in a flash of inspiration I came out with "*Seratus ribu*" – one hundred thousand – and said that this was 'last price'. He agreed.

He wrapped up the watches and shook me by the hand. I didn't know if this was because he had enjoyed the barter and admired my command of the language or if I'd been done. I smiled anyway – the transaction had cost me £5.

Pleased with my purchase, I wandered back to my bungalow. It was about 2pm (Saturday), therefore 7am in England. I thought this guaranteed that I would catch the family at home so I stopped at a telephone place – a *wartel* – where I was told that Saturdays were cheap rate – 5,000Rp per minute. The family were in and I had a brief conversation about my trip so far. Mum was very pleased to hear from me but I felt completely uninterested in any events at home after the sensory overload of the last few days and the anticipation of things to come. I returned to the bungalows, caught some sun for a couple of hours and watched ants preparing for the Trooping of the Colour on the parade ground of my verandah.

The friendly chap who ran the place didn't seem to be around so I gave up on the show idea and after a brief downpour wandered into town at about 7:00. I left the ants on manoeuvres in the shower room.

It seemed to be the night for numerous Balinese dance performances and as I walked the streets I passed choruses of singers, dancers and musicians. The top end of Monkey Forest Road was filled with the sound of gamelan and I peered into a temple area to see a dozen men creating haunting music with large drums, bronze xylophones, flutes and cymbals. The poorly lit streets enhanced the magical experience and I stood there, happy.

There were a couple of CD shops nearby and I popped in to find an album of Sundanese gamelan music, a particular one I'd seen played in a couple of restaurants. After a bite to eat I went to check if Anna had made it to Mandia. There was no news but at least I'd done the e-mail thing. I returned to the bungalows, packed and went to bed.

I'd been prevented from seeing Merapi but honoured with Bromo. I wondered what tomorrow would bring.

Negotiating a Volcano
(Gunung Batur)

Experience is not what happens to a man;
it is what a man does with what happens to him

I awoke at around 8.30 and the bus arrived promptly at 9.15. We did the classic Indonesian thing of driving around in circles for half an hour, being deposited in the middle of nowhere and getting on another bus. I'd grabbed a prime spot on the first bus but on the second was uncomfortably squashed amidst an overweight German family.

The bus journey was only around one and a half hours but, of course, didn't go where it was supposed to – Kintamani – but to Penelokan which was a few kilometres south. This wasn't a major problem as both were on the rim of the volcano. The main reason was probably to give trade to the bus driver's mate who owned a hotel down in the crater.

The view was incredible – a 10 kilometre wide caldera formed by two massive eruptions, the first around 25,000 years ago. Encircled by steep cliffs, it was now dominated by the unevenly flattened cone of Batur, marked with vents stretching down one side, one of which was gently smoking; to the right was a long crater lake, sparkling blue in the sunlight, which filled the east side of the caldera. Most of the land was filled with vegetation punctuated by small villages taking advantage of the rich soil and rich tourists. Batur itself, however, was a dusty brown apart from the massive lava flows caused by an eruption in 1974 which had blackened everything in their path. Thousands had been killed by its uneasy temperament over the years; the most recent major eruption had been in 1994 when lava fragments had been ejected to heights of 300 metres.

It looked like I had arrived on a peaceful day. A month earlier there had been a series of small eruptions for over a week; today, however, it was quietly smoking as inoffensively as it could.

As I sat admiring the view, people began to disperse and it wasn't long before a cheerful, smiling man approached me touting for business. Over his shoulder was the 2,000 metre peak of Gunung Abang sitting a few kilometres outside of the Batur caldera; in Indonesia, the word *gunung* is used to describe both mountains and volcanoes, as they tend to be pretty much the same thing. I had already made a tentative decision as to where to stay but the guy offered a free trip down to beside the lake where my climb would have to start and a room in his hotel for 20,000Rp – the hotel was, I think, the Hotel Segara, in the lakeside village of Kedisan. This all sounded okay so I got inside his Jeep and said "Hi" to a couple in the back.

"He got you too?" said the girl.

I grinned. "Looks that way."

We chatted as we were driven down the winding road to the lake. On arriving at the hotel we checked out the single-storey rooms that faced the central courtyard and agreed to stay. Just as we were getting settled we were collared by a friendly man offering trips up the volcano to see the sunrise – in his hand was a book of quotations from previous travellers about how good his trips were. They varied between $15 and $25 depending on the duration – four to seven hours – this was a price of around 240,000Rp, which compared extremely interestingly with my thirty-six hour Jogya-Bromo-Bali trip for 100,000Rp. He was very insistent that this was the only way to get up the volcano without getting lost (how you could lose this volcano, I didn't know) and that we needed to decide now. The three of us looked at each other and unspokenly agreed to mull it over during brunch. We made our excuses and went to order some food.

It now seemed appropriate to make some introductions. Vit and Diana were students from the Czech Republic studying English Language at university. Diana had spent a year in London as an au pair getting paid £30 per week; short dark hair framed her smiling face and her manner was a pleasant mix of eastern-European and English. Vit (pronounced 'veet') had light brown hair topping his gaunt frame and was less gregarious. They had both been working in Germany to save money for the trip and spoke very good English and German.

We chatted about getting up the volcano and very quickly decided that the hotel was asking an extortionate amount of money. We eventually came up with two options: one, hire a Jeep for twenty-four hours, go up this afternoon and, if we felt like it, tomorrow morning too, or two, charter transport to take us now.

The guy from the hotel hassled us again in a less friendly fashion than before and began to offer discounts; we left in search of a vehicle. We walked out of the hotel, the volcano just to our left and after five minutes we stopped a French guy in a Jeep and asked him where he'd acquired it. He pointed vaguely and told us that he'd paid $15 for two hours (which seemed an outrageous price). We carried on walking past various offers of guides and trips and came to a large parking area that seemed to be the main stop for boat journeys. An old guy asked us if we wanted a trip but we had heard warnings of the price changing halfway across the lake – we declined. We ambled through the car park and it wasn't long before we heard the traditional Indonesian greeting.

"Transport?"

Vit and Diana rolled their eyes as I turned to say, "We're looking for our own."

"You go to volcano?"

"Yes."

"I take you for seventy thousand."

We looked at each other – this could be a possibility.

"You need guide?"

"No, we want to go on our own."

"Okay. I take you there and wait."

We decided to have a brief discussion but in the few seconds we had been there, an audience of seven or eight locals had congregated in very close proximity. Bees round a honey pot, or as Indonesian's apparently say, "where there's sugar, there's ants" (*ada gula ada semut*). We tried to talk but the prods, interruptions and general presence around us was making it very difficult. We moved a few metres away and sat down; the crowd followed and surrounded us, unfriendly and unsmiling. Diana looked up and counted nine – had it been mild curiosity on their part, it would have been okay but there was something very uncomfortable and seemingly un-Balinese about the whole thing. We quietly discussed the options, occasionally asking interfering locals not to be so rude with their slightly aggressive and constant interruptions. Between three of us the offer could be quite a good idea so we asked for clarification of what it involved.

"You'll take us to the track and wait for us for around four hours and then bring us back?"

The driver agreed. We decided to haggle and offered him 50,000Rp; this was met with a tirade of how this was a good price, the last price, etc, etc. So much for bartering. The crowd were still around us and the whole thing felt a little intimidating. We decided to do the trip this afternoon, maybe catch the sunset at the top and probably not bother with sunrise. We confirmed the arrangements with the driver once more and asked him to drop us at the hotel for ten minutes so we could get changed, etc. As we left, faces were pressed ominously against the van like a scene from a low-budget horror movie.

Having got ready I was first to return to the van; the driver, crisp white shirt and big sunglasses, introduced himself as Wayan. We set off along the winding narrow road that skirted the base of the volcano. Wayan asked us if we wanted the short or medium walk; aware of the time constraints, we went for the shorter one. We drove through Toya Bungkah and eventually reached the slightly grubby village of Songan. The road took an abrupt and narrow left in the centre and we had to do some fancy manoeuvres to avoid several farm trucks. I was quite keen to stop and buy a little food and drink as I'd only had a pancake all day but due to my eagerness to get to the starting point and unwillingness to delay my companions I didn't say anything.

A couple of kilometres out of Songan we turned left down a farm track and stopped about one kilometre later at a collection of houses. Wayan vaguely pointed up the volcano.

"The track up that way. If you want you can go up and back down this way or you can come back the longer way to the hot springs (in Toya Bungkah) and I meet you there."

We weren't sure how long we wanted to walk for and thought it might be asking for trouble to meet Wayan elsewhere so we agreed to come back here. During this time a crowd of locals has gathered around the van and had been incessantly trying to talk to us. A little kid thrust his hand through the window (it was open).

"Hello, you need guide and I can offer you special price. We have three trips fifteen dollars, twenty dollars, twenty-five dollars…"

We smiled at each other wryly.

"Yes, we know. Thank you. Don't need guide."

We got out of the van and were once again surrounded with offers of guides that we tried politely to ignore. I spotted a food stall and thought now would be a good time to grab a drink and maybe a bite to eat.

"You want drink?" said the woman sitting behind it.

"How much?" I replied pointing at the coke.

"Ten thousand," said the little kid.

I laughed at the over-inflated price, "and the water?" I pointed to a small bottle normally costing 1,000Rp.

"Ten thousand," said the little kid.

"No really. How much?"

"Ten thousand."

"Okay, forget it then. I'm not that thirsty."

We set off in what we thought was vaguely the right direction, past a couple of lads chopping at wood with their parangs, but were quickly surrounded by five or six locals.

"Hey you need guide, you need guide."

"No we don't," we replied, "that's why we come this way."

"You get lost. Very difficult."

I pointed to the peak. "Look it's there. Exactly how difficult can it be?"

We continued walking.

The pack got more and more animated and at this point an older guy in dark trousers and a shirt started jumping in front of us.

"Hey you need guide. Only twenty dollars."

"We don't need guide. We don't want guide. We want to go on our own. Thank you."

The guy got more intense.

"Hey, look, stop. We talk. You need guide."

We carried on.

He began to harangue Vit and Diana who were just behind me and they did their best to politely decline; when this didn't work they ignored him. He jumped in front of me again.

"Hey stop. You need guide."

I stopped and looked at him.

"I'm sorry. We want to go on our own. We don't want a guide. Okay. Thank you."

We continued.

He jumped in front of me again and tried to grab my arm. The rest of the group continued to buzz around and the whole thing began to get very heated and slightly threatening as I noticed the sun catch the edge of the parang that one of them was carrying at his side. I couldn't quite understand what was being said at this point but it was something like, "Hey, this not your country, this our village, I make path, you can't go this way," etc, etc.

I replied as calmly and assertively as I could. "We would like to walk up the mountain. Thank you."

The guy became absolutely furious. He hit me with a tirade of abuse and the rest of the group got more and more animated. This was something I had never experienced in my years of travelling and it was very, very uncomfortable. It was turning into a rather ugly scene. My gut reaction was to carry on but I could see Vit and especially Diana were even more uncomfortable than I was.

Diana spoke. "We're not paying twenty dollars for a guide when we don't want one."

"Okay. Okay. Ten dollars."

"No, thank you."

"Okay. One hundred thousand." (A couple of weeks' wages.)

I laughed. "No way. Why should we? We can go ourselves."

The guy went nuts again until his younger apprentice stepped in quietly with an attempt at being amicable.

"Hey, I take you. Good price."

By now we'd walked some distance but though it seemed like a while it had probably only been three or four minutes.

"Okay, you give me eighty thousand Rupiah."

Diana spoke to Vit and looked at me, saying, "What about fifty thousand?"

It was impossible for us to discuss the situation in the presence of such a hostile audience, so I asked them if they spoke French. They didn't, and I didn't speak German. I really wasn't keen on paying anything but the situation was very unpleasant. The apprentice spoke to Diana.

"I take you for fifty thousand."

We stopped and looked at each other; it was seeming like we had little choice. We reluctantly agreed.

Suddenly it was all hypocritical smiles and the irate guy shook us by the hand and thanked us. My immediate English reaction was to shake his hand and smile but afterwards I regretted it deeply. To put it into perspective we were paying someone 50,000Rp (one week's average wages) for two hours work which we didn't need. Comparing that to the $40 per week a schoolteacher was paid in Indonesia and it seemed obscene.

Our 'guide' was a younger, quieter, eighteen-year-old called Mali. I got the impression that he was quite embarrassed by the whole thing. I wondered how much of the 50,000Rp he would see. We were accompanied by his mate with the parang, the little kid from the village, and an even smaller friend of his. The little kid told us his name but I wasn't interested and mentally referred to him as Macauley. He was twelve years old, spoke excellent English – sometimes with an Australian accent – and was extremely precocious.

We set off up the initially gentle slopes at quite a gallop; the kids talking incessantly. We put the unpleasantness behind us as we didn't want it to spoil what was supposed to be an exciting day. After about twenty minutes, the terrain steepened and our pace had slackened. We stopped for a brief rest and admired the fantastic views – in front of us the parched grassy ascent which led up to the rim of Batur; behind us the long slopes, partly covered in fir and deciduous trees, leading back to the village; the lake in the distance and the sheer cliffs surrounding us on all sides. Macauley pulled a bottle of coke from his bag – so this was why he was here.

"You want drink?"

"How much?"

"You pay at bottom."

"Not ten thousand I don't."

"Maybe later, okay?"

I shrugged in a non-committal fashion – I wasn't interested in getting fleeced by a twelve-year-old, regardless of how thirsty I was. This was aided by the fact that Vit had rather intelligently brought a large bottle of water from which we drank a small amount.

We continued up the steep, dusty, rocky track; the kids still talking incessantly. They asked me if I was married and I gave the appropriate Balinese answer of "not yet".

"You want to buy wife?" asked Macauley's small friend.

I laughed. "No, do you?"

Everyone started chuckling.

I looked at him again and asked. "Are you married?"

"Oh yes," he said.

"And you have children?"

"Three children."

Macauley joined in. "Monkey children. They live in the forest."

Everyone cracked up. We discussed his monkey children for a while and then got on to ages – he told us he was fifty and I told him I was seventy. They seemed to enjoy making things up and would finish sentences with "only kidding mate" or "no worries".

We were still going at quite a pace but were beginning to tire; Diana visibly so. We stopped more frequently (each time I was offered a drink from Macauley) and I used these opportunities to look around and take a number of photos. The village was now far below us, set amongst a browny-green patchwork of fields and trees.

The terrain was now quite steep and the intermittent trees gave way to clumps of wiry grass that spread out either side of the dirt track. We had only been walking for around an hour but the pace had been quick and the mid-afternoon sun had been hitting us hard the whole way. We began to notice sparse clouds below us moving around the lake; we were now within ten minutes of the summit. Our steps got heavier but eventually the ground began to level off and we were on the rim.

The first thing I noticed was a couple of benches that had been strategically positioned there; I fell onto one with a groan. The rest of the group soon joined me and we finally took in the magnificent view: the long route down to the village, the lake stretching itself around the cone, the sheer cliffs in the distance, and, of course, the crater. Several hundred metres in diameter, the uneven rim trailed round to the west and south, its inner walls partly covered by scrub. To the south-east, the crater fell away and in the distance I could see black lava flows looking like an oil slick on a brown sea. The uneven floor of the cone was around 40 metres below me, largely covered by scrubby grass but with steam emanating from a number of cracks around the inner edge of the rim. I moved away from the group to gain some personal space and take in the scene.

Macauley began to hover, his bag open and three bottles of coke in his hand.

"You want drink now?"

"Not if they're ten thousand."

"Okay, okay, I give you good price – eight thousand."

I laughed and said, "No way". Macauley looked sullen and gave a speech about carrying them all the way up the mountain; my lack of sympathy wasn't difficult to spot.

"How about twenty thousand for three," said Diana.

"I'm not going to pay him seven thousand," I replied.

"Look we'll get them," she said. "Pay us five thousand."

I should have felt guilty at this point for being so tight, but I didn't. Macauley wasn't happy with the price but opened the drinks with a sullen expression, muttering under his breath. He then asked us if we'd pay some money so that he could give one to the guide and at this point we gave him a polite version of "fuck off, stop taking the piss". He sat and sulked on the bench cursing loudly in

Balinese; mostly, I thought, directed at me. It was strange – he'd told me I was his best friend twenty minutes earlier. I later learned an Indonesian proverb, *"habis manis sepah dibuang"* – "after the sweetness the remains are discarded". I didn't mind being discarded.

We drank the coke and I asked Mali about the empty stalls that lay a few metres from the bench. He said they served drinks as it got very busy up here at sunrise – this morning there had apparently been nearly one hundred people. I was now very glad I'd come at this time of day. It was clear, if a little hazy, and the hot afternoon sun was calmed by a slight breeze. Beautiful, and we were the only ones impetuous enough to be up here in the middle of the day. The only thing spoiling it was the kids who seemed to be getting noisier and noisier. My main reason for wanting to come up on my own was to experience the quiet and take everything in. At 1717 metres above sea level, it was by no means the highest volcano in Indonesia; but the way in which it rose 700 metres (over 2,000 feet) from the caldera floor with the calm lake at its feet and the distant cliffs surrounding it made it a truly wonderful place.

Vit, Diana and I were in awe of the whole scene, but those accompanying us seemed quite bored by it. I wondered how many times you had to climb up here before that happened. They obviously wanted to move on so we asked about following the narrow rim to the other side and perhaps looking at the remains of the still smoking crater which erupted in 1994. Macauley, who seemed to speak for the group, said this could be done but it would cost more – surprise, surprise. This would have given us the option of taking the long way down but we had already arranged where to meet our driver so we decided to wander round the rim as far as we could and then return the same way. Mali agreed to take us and thankfully the entourage stayed where they were.

As we walked, Mali gently pointed out the occasional feature and actually seemed like a really nice guy. He quietly led us up to a higher part of the rim and we approached the area where steam was rushing out of the rocks, blown by the wind. He showed us a place two metres down from the edge where it was possible to cook eggs and we tentatively placed our hands against the rock to feel the heat. Mali took a chunk of red lava, scarred with yellow sulphur stains, for me to keep. We then took a few photos of each of us standing inside a volcano, the steep brown walls above and below us, rocky and scrub-covered, and the gusts of steam shooting out over the rim.

We climbed back up and continued our progress past the rushing steam. The rim was now sheer on both sides; to continue we moved to the outer edge and had to precariously find hand and footholds in the rock. Standing on the rim again, I asked for a photo to be taken and as I looked either side of me realised how steep it really was – a tumble of several hundred metres down the outer rim and a thirty to forty metre drop into the crater. We carefully moved on and after a further ten minutes reached the far side where we were able to see the kids as specks sitting on the bench – this gave a real sense of scale so I took a couple of pictures. We could now get a better view of the plume of white smoke from a smaller, flattened cone further on and around us we could see the solidified lava flows stretching out in all directions across the floor of the basin. It was a very impressive sight. We had a fantastic view of the whole area and sat quietly transfixed by it. Clouds moved around below us and it was all so peaceful.

Mali didn't seem that interested in sitting there for ages admiring the view so we briefly discussed the idea of sending him off with the 50,000Rp and making our own way back when we felt like it. This seemed to be a good plan so we told him of our intentions and he seemed quite pleased that he could go early.

However, he then quietly said, "You give me ten thousand for taking you to here?"

We looked at each other in unspoken agreement.

"No," said Vit, "sorry but we agreed a price and you didn't mention anything about paying more."

Mali shrugged his shoulders and we gave him the 50,000Rp. He bid us farewell and set off at a canter around the rim. We felt a little guilty as he was actually a nice guy and we wondered how much he would actually get to keep. However, we were still smarting from the events earlier and had a good old bitch about everything that had happened. But now we were happily on our own as intended. There was complete silence all around, broken only occasionally by the movement of the clouds. It was fantastic being somewhere so big and having it all to ourselves. We sat there for a long while watching drifting layers of muslin moving in and then away to reveal the crater floor below. The clouds around us quickened their pace and at times would rush towards and through us, bringing a chill for a few minutes until the equatorial sun broke through again – it was entrancing being in a cloud.

The cool muslin built up in layers and stretched its way over the rim until we could just make out the shapes of rocks a few metres away; this did nothing but add to the magic of the place. After a few minutes we realised that the clouds were probably here to stay and it might be worth starting to make a move. We walked carefully round the rim, stopping once or twice to take precarious-looking photographs but there was now little to see below us. Back at our original spot, we sat for a while wondering if the skies would clear enough for us to see the sunset. After half an hour or so it didn't seem likely and it had gone 5pm. It seemed sensible to start heading back down. As we descended we came through the cloud to see the village below us; looking back, the top thirty metres of volcano was now completely hidden. We stopped halfway down for a brief rest and then continued our descent at a relatively rapid rate down the dusty track.

It was dark as we approached the village. Macauley was there, sitting on a motorbike. He bid us a cheery hello and then drove off.

We walked the last kilometre through small farms with small collections of kids shouting "hello" over and over again – celebrity status achieved. Wayan was still there waiting. The grinning Macauley caught us again.

"You want drink? Three thousand?"

My head said 'Fuck off.' My mouth smiled and said, "No, thank you."

As we got into the truck he held out his hand, I assumed for a handout – we ignored it.

Wayan laughed as we told him what had happened. We couldn't decide whether he'd set us up or not but we gave him the benefit of the doubt.

After the Sweetness
(Batur and buses)

Where there's carcasses, there's crocodiles

Back at the hotel we grabbed a shower and met for dinner. We'd intended to find somewhere else but there didn't seem to be much around so we decided to eat at the hotel. We grabbed a table near the lake and sat shivering in the cool evening breeze of the mountain; I went back to my room and put a sweatshirt on. We beckoned to one of the waiters who ambled over, indifferently.

"Could we have a menu please?"

"You want food?" he replied sullenly.

"Yes please."

He grunted and shuffled off. We got our menus and perused them slowly whilst chatting about the day. The waiter returned.

"Ready?" he said in voice which sounded more like "I have held your sister hostage and will kill her if you do not meet my demands".

"Oh sorry," we said, smiling, "can you give us another minute?"

He huffed something in Indonesian and walked off. We looked at each other, trying to fathom what the hell was up with him. We all settled on fish – two with rice, one with fries. Another waiter in a baseball cap and leather jacket came over.

"Yes?"

We smiled and gave him our order but Diana still wasn't quite sure what fish to have. After five seconds the waiter turned his back on us with a bored look and as we raised our eyebrows at each other he walked off to the other side of the room. I laughed.

"This is bloody ridiculous."

"I just want to walk out," said Diana.

I don't think any of us had ever experienced such rudeness – it had to be a fit of pique over the fact that we weren't going to take their sunrise trip. Baseball cap returned and we gave him the rest of the order. As he turned to go I gave him a childish, patronising smile which he didn't see but brought Diana out in a fit of giggles; we couldn't believe this place – everything about Bali and the Balinese was being shot to bits. The fish arrived – two small fried whole fish covered in sauce, very bony with very little meat. We assumed our chips would follow closely but after five minutes felt the need to ask. The chips duly arrived. It was another five minutes later when Vit piped up.

"I wonder where my rice is?"

I was too busy trying to separate bones and meat in my mouth to reply, but grunted to acknowledge. I wonder which part of hell involves an eternity of having small fish bones stuck in that area where your teeth and gums meet. Another waiter wandered by and Vit wryly asked whether it would be appropriate to have the rice with the meal. I think the sardonic humour was lost on the waiter but Vit got his rice. By this time I was finished and was poking around in my mouth with my fingers.

After dinner we discussed the day, how excellent the mountain had been and how crap we'd been treated. The attitude of the hotel staff had really rounded it off for us and we discussed contacting Lonely Planet about our experiences. Diana was particularly vociferous about this and I learned the next day that it was because the waiters were listening in to our conversation. We announced that we were leaving early tomorrow. Surprisingly waiter number one responded.

"If you want to go to top of hill, get public bus and don't pay more than two hundred Rupiah."

We nearly fell over with shock at his helpfulness; we turned, smiled and thanked him. The next day we realised that helpfulness was not the appropriate word.

We paid for dinner and wandered outside to look at the beautiful black sky and the myriad of stars. On the ridge of the volcano we could see a red glow. Excited, we realised that it must be from the smoke we saw this afternoon and we grinned with pleasure. We arranged to meet at around 9:00 the next morning and I mentioned unrealistically that I might get up for sunrise, not at all expecting to.

I awoke at 6:00. I lay there for a couple of minutes, amazed at myself and wondering whether or not it would be worth getting up. As I was awake, I thought I might as well, so I got dressed and wandered out into the cool morning.

The glow from the volcano was visible to the north, to the west the moon was bright and to the east, behind the cliffs, it was getting light. I walked down the road and took a narrow mud track leading down to the shore. In front of me, the shadow of Batur rose from the lake, the child of two massive primeval volcanoes, one of which was now filled by the gentle water lapping at my feet. A fisherman sat hunched in his boat; it was very quiet.

Twenty minutes on it was getting lighter and people were beginning to go about their business – a woman glided past me with a plastic bucket to collect water from the lake and a farmer slowly sauntered into his smallholding and began to gently poke at the earth around his crops. The light on the volcano was constantly changing and I took several photos trying to capture the shifting shadows and the shades of brown and gold. As the sun rose above the cliffs, boats were silhouetted in the water and Batur looked at its most impressive, its uneven shape allowing a view into the shadowy crater we had crept around yesterday.

The sound of the lake was broken by the dut-dut-dut-dut-dut of a small petrol engine. Over it was crouched the farmer, carefully adjusting a plastic hose which led down to the lake and was now irrigating his land. I mentally faded the sound and merged it into the overall sensory picture of the place.

I had been there over an hour and it was now fully light so I wandered back to the hotel, past groups of smartly-dressed kids on their way to school. I ordered my free breakfast of coffee and a pancake from a peevish member of staff and then caught up on my diary. Vit and Diana appeared at around 8:30 and we were all ready to go an hour later. We had paid our bill the night before so we walked out without any farewells and ambled down to the crossroads. Thanks to the advice from the waiter at the hotel we were going to stick rigidly to 200Rp.

Our first offer of transport was 2,000Rp each so we offered him 200Rp and he drove off grumpily. We were quite happy to wait for public transport. A bemo arrived with a few uninterested locals huddled on its bench seats and offered to take us for 1,000Rp each – still too much so we declined. A second one came by, empty – we didn't really haggle but got 2500Rp for all of us. The restaurant owner on the corner stepped in to tell us this was a good deal but we didn't believe him, and anyway this was beginning to be fun – so many times we had felt fleeced and too often had been forced into paying a price through either false information or desperation; when you're not actually in a hurry and you don't care whether you get to your destination or not it can be quite liberating.

Squabbling over 10p is one of those travelling clichés that is difficult to understand until you've been in the situation. In some cases, it can be the traveller simply being tight but I think that generally it is the acknowledgement of the value of money in the country you are in and an awareness of the relative prices of things.

For example, paying an untrained guide more money in a day than a policeman may get paid in a week only helps encourage more untrained people to become guides, and corruption in the police force. Any tourist who thinks that they should pay local people extra money because they can afford it should think more about the effects on the local economy and the view that this gives of Westerners.

Each driver that went by expected us to capitulate and I believe was quite shocked by our resistance. A guy on a motorbike stopped next to us and insistently asked where we were going.

"Up the hill."

"Ya, but where?"

"We don't know."

He reeled off a number of possible destinations and we shrugged at each one. He drove off unsatisfied. A half-full bemo pulled over.

"How much to the top?"

"Ten thousand."

We fell over in giggles at the price.

"How much you pay?"

In a heap on the ground, we couldn't get any words out and he drove off, unimpressed.

Twenty minutes had gone by now and we wondered if we were breaking some kind of record – we certainly felt we were making some kind of point, albeit childish. The motorbike guy stopped right by us again and sat motionless – the three of us chatted loudly about our experiences in Batur and how people wouldn't leave you alone and how rude we found it. We were probably too subtle but he left shortly afterwards. By now the man in the restaurant felt we were lowering the tone of the neighbourhood and when an empty van drove by and asked us if we wanted a lift, he stepped in and said 3,000Rp for the three of us would be a good price; we looked at each other and decided we'd had some kind of Pyrrhic victory. We were up at the top within ten minutes.

Looking back at the Batur caldera I wondered what it was like before it had been corrupted by the influence of tourism and how the genuine guides, wherever they were, coped with the charlatans who were out to make as much money in as short a space of time as possible. But perhaps the people had always possessed this aggressive self-interest; perhaps that is what living in the shadow of an active volcano does to you; or perhaps it was simply a symptom of the wider problems going on in the country. The caldera had created its own culture of people living on their wits and on what the land could provide. The tourists were the occasional pieces of meat thrown to them, and in the words of one saying, *adakah buaya menolak bangkai?* Is there a crocodile that would turn down a carcass?

We decided to get a public bus to Padangbai via Klungkung; we ignored the offers of chartered transport and I went to practise my Indonesian on a lady in a café. I bought a coke and asked her about the buses. She said one would be along in about five minutes and would cost 2,000 – 3,000Rp. She was right and we were soon on our way.

Diana and I chatted for most of the long journey and on our arrival at Klungkung we got on a packed bus to Padangbai. Diana and Vit got a seat together and I got to look after the three backpacks at the back. As we approached Padangbai I handed the conductor 9,000Rp for the three of us; the bus stopped and I started unloading – there was a call from Vit.

"No, we're carrying on."

"Oh," I said "Okay. I've just paid for us."

Vit scrambled around for some money but didn't have it in any place he could access. In the meantime there was a sense of urgency from the conductor which is never present when it comes to timetables or anything else for that matter, except, apparently, when it comes to getting on and off buses.

"Another time," I yelled and all I saw was Diana waving from the window.

Top: The view from Borobudur
Bottom: Prambranan

Above: Semeru
Below: Nick on the rim of Bromo

Left: A temple in Ubud
Below: Batur

Above: Padangbai beach
Below: Boats at Padangbai

Above: Stickfighting
Below: Nick at the Rinjani campsite

Above: The Rinjani caldera
Below: Nick

Continuing Eastwards
(Bali to Lombok)

"I give you good price"

My backpack sat, unceremoniously discarded, by the side of the empty road. I brushed off the dust and optimistically picked it up in the hope that transport would appear; a few seconds later a brown bemo came shooting around the corner and offered to take me to the beach and port area. It was 2pm and full of kids who had just finished school. I bid them *"Selamat siang"* and got a hearty chorus of *"Siang"* back as I squeezed into the hot interior and sat down. A few asked me where I was from but the rest just grinned at me with interest.

At the port I was immediately approached by a man with the offer of a room. It was a very cheap 5,000Rp with breakfast and was okay but I'd already planned on a place called Kerti Inn, mentioned in Lonely Planet, which was on the beach. I told him I was meeting a friend but would return if she wasn't there; another one of the tiny lies you tell when trying not to offend.

Padangbai was a small fishing port in a bay with a pretty white sand beach, small town centre and rows of restaurants and guesthouses. Its largest asset, however, is the ferry terminal from where the four and a half hour ferry to Lombok sailed every two hours. I wandered along the beach-front and arrived at

Kerti – a collection of small bungalows and larger, two-storey huts punctuated by tall palm trees. A teenage girl welcomed me and led me to a pleasant bungalow style room with en-suite shower that was 20,000Rp with breakfast included. I asked her if she'd accept 15,000. She referred this to her boss who became quite animated. I could see she was a little offended so I relented and told her I'd love to take it. She smiled and I dumped my stuff on the bed. After yesterday's adventures and my early morning I was feeling pretty tired, even though it was only mid-afternoon.

An interesting feature of all Indonesian guest houses is the incredibly detailed government forms one is required to fill out on checking in:

- Port of embarkation. (What exactly does that mean?)
- Port of arrival.
- Where are you going?
- When are you going?
- Why are you here? (Philosophy on guest house forms, whatever next?)
- Occupation. (This started off as lecturer but I went through several career changes as the trip progressed and ended up as an astronaut – part of me hoped to be in a fatal accident and the press to report the story based on information gleaned from my guest house records.)
- First primary school.
- Sexual partners since the age of sixteen.
- Who would play you in a Hollywood version of your life?
- I may have begun to exaggerate.

I grabbed a drink and wandered over to the beach. I'd been in Indonesia for well over a week (it seemed like a month, but in a good way) and this was the first time I'd seen a proper beach. Colourful fishing boats stretched left and right and a strong breeze blew off the sea. A lady with an armful of sarongs parked herself on the white sand next to me and started chatting in confident English. She asked me where I was from, what I was doing here, etc, and I was quite happy to talk to her about my trip and find out a little about her daily commute to Padangbai from the nearby town of Giagur. When she learnt I was from England, she produced a £1 coin and a 10p piece.

"Where did you get those?" I asked with some surprise. The last time I'd seen 'foreign' coins was in Jogya when some kids at the guest house showed me their coin collection.

"I sell sarong to English lady. She give me this instead of ten thousand Rupiah."

"A good deal," I said, "maybe worth eighteen thousand."

"You want to buy?" she asked.

I laughed. "Not really. I don't really need."

"How much you give?"

"Well, maybe seventeen thousand but I don't really want."

"No. Worth twenty thousand," she said, clearly fully aware of the ups and downs of the foreign exchange markets (as was evident in any Indonesian town where grocers, clothes shops and restaurants can offer you exchange rate deals precisely based on the daily currency movements in London and New York).

"Well, maybe, but I don't really want. I'm travelling, don't need English money."

We chatted about other stuff for a while and then she asked. "You want sarong?"

I really couldn't be bothered with trade negotiations right now and anyway I'd promised myself that I wouldn't buy anything until the end of my trip. It was time for another tiny lie.

"Not really, I have two already."

"Where you buy them?"

"Er, one in Bangkok and one in Ubud."

"How much you pay?"

"Can't remember."

"Good quality, like this?" she said, pointing to one.

"One is good quality, the other very thin," I embellished.

She showed me a very nice blue and green sarong with a price of 60,000Rp that quickly dropped to 40,000. Another time I might have bought one from her and I now regret it; but at that moment I couldn't be bothered, which was a shame as she was nice and business was obviously slow.

A friend of hers spotted us and wandered over. Realising where I was from, she produced £1.20 she wanted me to buy – I'd never pictured myself as a travelling bureau de change. I politely declined. She asked me why and I told her I didn't need to carry English money for the next three weeks so we made small talk for a while until I began to get hungry.

I asked the sarong lady if she would be there tomorrow as in the back of my mind I was still thinking about maybe buying from her but she said she wasn't sure; I looked for her the next day with no success. I made my excuses to them and went back to Kerti to get changed as I was still in the trousers I had worn for the bus journey here.

All of the beachfront cafes were offering fresh fish – tuna, swordfish, shark and marlin. I sat down at the first one I encountered and decided to have fish and chips. I asked the young waitress what her favourite fish was – she pointed at the marlin on the menu and so that's what I chose. It was the strangest battered fish and chips I'd had – the fish was the strong meaty consistency I'd expected but was also cut in the classic south-east Asian ad hoc way which meant that periodically it would include a fin.

After lunch I walked slowly into the main part of the small town to get some information on times and costs of getting to Lombok. The ferry was 5,000Rp to locals and 7,000Rp to others. For 20,000Rp I could get to Sengiggi – the main beach resort and for 21,000Rp to Bangsal for the Gili Islands. I definitely wanted to do the Gilis but it had also been recommended that I go to Lendang Nangka in the middle of the island to stay at the house of a local teacher, Hadji Radiah and get a sense of rural life with the Sasak people of Indonesia. It was all a question of time and I was still strongly drawn to the idea of an encounter with the massive Rinjani volcano which, based on what I had read and heard, sounded like a fantastic challenge but something that would need some serious planning. I decided to think about it and sort it out that evening. After a quick stop at the local grocers where I haggled for some film for my camera and bought a large bottle of water, I wandered back to my bungalow.

I thought it would be good to catch some sun so I grabbed a towel and went to find an allegedly nice cove ten minutes from the town. I assumed it was on the other side of the headland to the north, so I followed the road and then took a path upwards into the woods. There was a large Balinese temple, which I circumnavigated and I followed a track around the cliff-top with views of the dark green hills surrounding Padangbai and the animated blue waters beyond the bay. I spotted the cove and continued along the path until I noticed some steps leading downwards into the cliff. I can never resist steps so I headed down and there in the cliff face was a small shrine dotted with small parcel gifts, I assumed as some kind of offerings to the spirits of the seas. I retraced my steps and continued through the wood. Eventually I came to a wider track that led down to the pretty cove where a couple of people were sitting. The tide was coming in and the mid-afternoon sun only partly lit up the sand. I continued on to see if there was another cove beyond here. Tracks followed the edge of the cliff-top but on the other side was just a rocky shoreline. I passed a local sitting deep in thought and found a place to rest in the sunshine and watch the waves crashing against the cliffs. Clouds were building up to the north-west over the island and seemed to be moving towards me; this, however, was completely at odds with the stiff breeze coming in off the sea from the south-east. I was perplexed by the meteorological reasons for this but more importantly for me the clouds quickly blotted out the sun. After fifteen minutes I decided to trek back.

The sky began to brighten as I approached Kerti – it was now around 5:00 and I sat on the beach watching kids playing football. As dusk approached I had a shower and contemplated the next couple of weeks with the aid of my Lonely Planet and an old guide book that was sitting on a bookshelf by reception. I counted back where I needed to be when and quickly realised that even though Lombok was half the size of Bali, travelling around was likely to be just as time-consuming and I wasn't going to fit everything in. I'd have to miss out on the beaches of the south and the Sasak culture of the centre. The decision was made: a ticket to the west coast town of Sengiggi, stay one night and then attempt Rinjani. At over 3,700 metres (12,000 feet) high, with a 6.5 by 8 kilometre caldera, 1,500 metre high cliffs, and a massive crater lake, it sounded incredible. From what I could gather, the climb up to the rim was difficult; a steep trek through forest to a point around 3,000 metres above sea level. However, there was apparently an even tougher climb to the summit; a four day expedition involving an exhausting and risky struggle up steep rocky slopes. It seemed that few people took this arduous journey to the summit and there had been the odd fatality. I was excited at the prospect of seeing this place.

I walked into town, bought the ticket and then went for food. That evening I intended to catch up on my diary and walked into one of the open-sided restaurants just off the beach with a cheerful "Table for one, please".

"Sure come and sit with this guy. He's a kiwi," the boss said with a smile.

I didn't want to be churlish so I plonked myself down and said "Hi". He wasn't really a kiwi – he was Balinese but had created a career of travelling through New Zealand picking fruit. He now wasn't far away from NZ citizenship that would then pretty much enable him to work anywhere. We chatted about Bali and Lombok and I asked him about Rinjani. He recommended it and advised me to get to Senaru or Batu Koq at the foot of the mountain and find some Javanese who were climbing it as they would probably be happy for me to join them and it would be a lot cheaper. At any rate he said I should be able to do it for a lot less than the $40 and other fees quoted. We were joined briefly by an Aussie and American friend of his and shared stories about our adventures so far; they were unsurprised at my Batur experiences. I then had some excellent swordfish and before long a couple of hours had passed. I didn't want to be rude but I really needed to do some writing so I made my excuses and left. I sauntered across to the restaurant opposite and ordered a pancake and coffee. I stayed there for about an hour and then went to bed.

I was up at around 9am and had papaya, toast and coffee on the porch. Checkout was rather annoyingly at 10am so I quickly packed and dumped my bag at reception. I had to pick up my tickets at 11:30 for the 12:00 ferry. I thought I'd briefly try to catch some sun so I lay on the beach for around forty minutes, picked up my stuff, got the tickets and quickly walked to the ferry. I walked through the car deck, up two flights of stairs to a collection of around sixty seats at the front of the ship under cover. I made myself comfortable whilst trying to ignore the dozens of hawkers selling everything from newspapers to pineapple to rice. I then watched people getting on, easily spotting random British people due to their manner and their clothes – shiny shorts and sports tops are often the giveaway.

The ferry departed and I took a couple of photos of the bay from a narrow gangway where I stood for a while watching the coast of Bali. I then sat back down to have a rummage for my headphones; the trip was supposed to be four hours but I was betting on five. The water became progressively choppier as we got further from shore and after about an hour we were bumping around with waves crashing against the front of the ship and a strong wind blowing in our faces. I was in the extreme right front seat and would periodically feel spray on my face. This was fine until a massive wave hit the ship and the remains of it hit me. I turned to a German couple sitting next to me and made the observation that this was getting silly. I got up and moved myself and my belongings to the middle. I then decided to go for a brief wander around the ship but after a couple of minutes noticed a movement of people from the front to the inside. Wandering out to see what was going on, I saw five rows of seats covered in water – my bag was the last remaining evidence of human habitation. It was wet but okay. I dragged it to the back row of seats and sat down.

Halfway through the journey, and unannounced, we crossed the Wallace line. Sir Alfred Wallace, a 19th century naturalist (not naturist, as someone tried to point out) observed great differences in flora and fauna between Bali and Lombok. He put this down to the ice age when sea levels were lower but the deep Lombok strait remained a sea barrier; he concluded, therefore, that this marked a clear divide between Asia and Australasia and it helped inform the new and radical theory of evolution.

I ate a banana and had a snooze as rest of the journey passed by uneventfully. The sea had calmed a little and I wandered up to the open top deck in the hope of getting some photographs but it was much too hazy. A few backpackers were taking in the sun and I chatted to a Dutch girl for about an hour until we entered the large calm bay of Lembar at exactly 4:30. A crowd assembled on the car deck to be first out and another crowd assembled on the wharf to be the first to sell them something. I took a short and precarious route down a rickety ladder and was met by a guy who was going to give me transport to Sengiggi as part of my ticket – there were around twelve of us in two minibuses. I was with the Dutch girl, a

Dutch guy she was travelling with, three Scots and two other guys who didn't really talk to people. The Scots were the three I identified as Brits at Padangbai – a guy with very blond highlights and two girls, all chatting away merrily.

I asked the Scottish guy where he was from.

"Scortlund," he replied.

"Yes," I said in a "I didn't need a roomful of cunning linguists to work that one out" kind of way, and a smile, "but where?"

He laughed. "Oh, near Aviemore."

I nodded sagely and tried to think of something interesting and non-ski-related to say about Aviemore. I couldn't.

"So, how long have you been travelling?"

Ahh, that wonderful question, the backpacker's equivalent of the first month at university when everyone asks "So what course are you on?". To be fair to first-year university students, though, the question has changed in the last ten years; it is now "So what course are you on?" but in an ironic voice. Nevertheless, the basic subtext hasn't changed, it still means "Let's go get pissed", or "fancy a shag?" Clearly that's not the case with "So, how long have you been travelling"; backpackers are too politically correct for that kind of behaviour (and I mean that ironically).

We all chatted for the hour or so it took to get to Sengiggi and we arrived just before 6:00. As an amazing coincidence we had all pretty much settled on the same guest house but when we arrived the place was full; it clearly hadn't occurred to me that if I based my accommodation choices on the same guidebook as everyone else there was an outside chance of this happening. A couple of touts approached us and we eventually followed a guy who said he had rooms for 12,000Rp. We walked for five minutes into town and down a track to a collection of small bungalows. We checked out the rooms, discovered that breakfast was included and I'd dumped my stuff and signed on the dotted line while the others were still deciding.

It was approaching 6.15 and my plan had been to make it to Sengiggi for sunset. I walked at a brisk pace towards the beach, cut through some open ground past a collection of goats and then through the lavish Sengiggi Beach Hotel. The beach was long with white sand and fringed with palm trees and restaurants. The sun had disappeared behind clouds as I wandered up to the breakwater at the south edge of the bay. A number of people were sitting on the steps and there appeared to be an unusual number of single Western females surrounded by Indonesian gigolos who were attempting to charm them.

I hoped to get a blaze of colour but the sunset ended with a bit of a whimper. I sat for a short while and then ambled back up the beach. A young guy selling sarongs approached me and said "Hi". He introduced himself as Ecu (what, another one?) and asked me about my plans for the next few days. I told him about my intention to climb Rinjani but my unwillingness to pay the earth. He told me he had a friend (of course he did) who wasn't anything to do with travel agents and who might be able to help me for around 300,000Rp. I thought about it as we wandered back to the bungalows and when I got there I asked him if he could sort something out this evening. He led me to the shop where his friend worked. He wasn't there but the owner sat me down and asked me about my plans. We discussed the option of going to the rim, hot springs and back in three days; going right to the top over four days or trying to shorten that to three. According to what I'd read in Lonely Planet, this would be really difficult. Four days would seriously curtail my chances of going to the Gili Islands. Ecu disappeared to find his friend and came back saying that there was a small group going tomorrow for 500,000Rp – this wasn't really what I wanted so I declined.

He walked with me back to the bungalows and asked me if I needed transport to Senaru.

"It depends on the price," I replied, guardedly.

He offered me the chance to take a motorbike all the way, stopping from time to time at waterfalls, etc.

"Do you have a motorbike?" I asked, as my experiences suggested that young guys with motorbikes tend not to do much walking around.

He said no but he could hire one for the day for about 15,000Rp. The total cost would be 25,000 to 30,000Rp – hardly anything for his time. My alternative was to either get a bus north to Bangsal, then to Bayan and then to get a bemo to Senaru or go south to the bus terminal at Sweta and go north from there. I was getting hungry at this point so I suggested we meet at 9:30 at the internet place and decide then.

The bungalows were quiet so I wandered back out and found a reasonable restaurant on the beach with quite a nice atmosphere but uncomfortable wooden chairs. I thought I'd try two classic Lombok dishes – deep fried crispy beef and hot and sour spinach and peanut soup. The food took ages to come but was great when it arrived, albeit the soup was a bit spicy and I noticed later that part of it had ended up as an artistic stain down my back. It was 9:30 by the time I left and I rushed to the internet place. I bumped into Ecu on the way and we discussed tomorrow's arrangements. I asked him if he would be able to take me up to the rim of the volcano but he said he had to work at a restaurant in the afternoon. We arranged for him to sort out the motorbike and to pick me up at 9:00. I offered to give him some money but he declined so we said farewell and I went to do some e-mailing. There were a number of messages waiting for me from a couple of friends from home and also Mike and Anna (who had eventually received the note I left at Mandia but only after a long conversation with someone who worked there about her boyfriend looking for her). I sent a few back and returned to the bungalows to get ready for whatever tomorrow would bring.

Finding Adventure
(finding Rinjani)

We do not climb a mountain because it is there,
we climb it because we are here

I awoke at 8:30, had breakfast and was ready to go before 9:00. Some of the people from the ferry were milling about so I had some brief chats. 9:00 came and went and I wandered out to the gate to see where my lift was. Nobody there so I wandered back. A few people made comments about Indonesian *jam karet* (rubber time) and I nodded in agreement. 9:30 came and went and an English guy appeared with a hangover. I made a comment about his obviously rough night and we chatted for a while. 10:00 arrived and that was my cut-off point; quite what had happened I didn't know but I couldn't wait around any longer. I wandered into town and tried to get a bemo going north to Bangsal – there were few public buses on this route and a couple of guys quoted me 20,000Rp. I soon realised I'd have to get on to one of the main bus routes and so took the forty minute bus journey south to Amphon (2,000Rp) and was guided onto a bemo (1,500Rp) which took me to the large bus terminal at Sweta.

I asked for the bus to Bayan or Anyar and was pointed in several directions; eventually two people agreed on the same direction and I walked over to a large decrepit shack with wheels. This was the local bus to Bayan – the final stop before Batu Koq and Senaru – and the cost for the two and a half hour journey was 3,000Rp (15p).

It had gone 11:00 and the bus was supposed to leave at 12:00. A helpful young guy befriended me and gave me all the details – I thought he was the conductor but it transpired he was travelling up to Anyar for some purpose or other. My backpack was unceremoniously dumped on the roof and with my small backpack over my shoulder I went off to get a drink with my new friend in tow. When we returned to the bus, there were still empty seats and it was only 11:20. He said the bus wouldn't leave until 12:00 and would I like him to take me to see the bird market over the road. I thought I might as well so we wandered over chatting on the way.

I didn't really know what to expect from a bird market but it was exactly what it said – hundreds of different kinds of birds up for sale. We passed live chickens in cages, ducks in sacks with just their heads sticking out, minah birds, parrots, cockatoos, hawks and many, many more exotic species – apparently birds were popular as pets. I asked how much a duck would cost.

"Why, you want one?" He asked, enthusiastically.

I quickly said I was just curious, worrying that I'd mistakenly entered into a verbal contract and wondering what I would do with a pet duck; even if I could get it home there would probably be an unfortunate incident with my neighbour's cat and we'd end up with a duck-filled fatty-puss. He told me the bill would be around 20,000Rp and I asked him how much the rest of the duck would cost. I then stopped embellishing real events with poor jokes about ducks.

The market was busy and there was a brisk trade in chickens going on – many people buying a single live specimen which would be placed in a small bamboo cage and then taken on a motorbike ride. After a few minutes we left the bird market and, unlike any of the chickens, crossed the road in order to get some fruit for the journey. A grocer had some rather nice looking grapes and oranges so I bought half a kilo of each for around 10,000Rp; probably too much but it was the first time I had spotted grapes in Indonesia and they were very good.

We were at the bus by 11:50 and I grabbed a seat by the door where I had some room to stretch out. The bus was packed by 12:00 and we trundled off. Within five minutes more people were piling on but with typical resourcefulness, Indonesians buses have a solution for this – movable seats which balance between each row. However, soon these were all full and there was also a collection of around five people jammed into the doorway – so much for me having some space. I spent an uncomfortable one and a half hours bouncing around but gradually as people reached their various destinations the bus emptied. Wayan (for that was his name) asked me about my plans and I told him I had an idea of where to stay and that I intended to climb Rinjani myself. He mentioned a cost of $30 but I didn't know if he meant that that was the price for arranging it directly in Senaru or the normal price from Sengiggi. He told me he knew of a good place to stay and that I should stick with him as there were some dodgy people around.

We arrived at the poor excuse for a bus terminal at Bayan, desolate was the word that sprang to mind, and my dusty backpack was handed down from the roof of the bus. A few local lads watched me carefully as I stood looking conspicuous until Wayan guided me to a bemo that would cost 1,500Rp to Senaru. There was some discussion with the locals whom I think wanted a piece of the action but Wayan dealt with it and told me to ignore them. It felt like the middle of nowhere and was consequently a little intimidating so I was happy when the bemo set off and wound its way up the mountain – young guys, young girls, old women, various items of shopping, five bags of cement and one Englishman. As we passed through Batu Koq it was about 3:00 and Wayan informed me there would be stick fighting at 4:00 – a very popular local event. He told me I should go but this was slightly at odds with my plan to see the nearby waterfalls. I said I'd think about it. We eventually got to a guest house, Gunung Baru, and I checked Lonely Planet which didn't mention it. Its collection of huts looked pretty nice though; 8,000Rp including breakfast and relatively near the beginning of the trail. I agreed to stay.

I was shown to a sparse room, with connecting bathroom, opposite the raised dining area. I dumped my stuff on the bed and returned to order a coke and a pancake. The wonderful thing about backpacking in south-east Asia; you can always get a pancake. Wayan was seated in conversation with an older guy who quickly turned to me.

"So, you want to climb the mountain."

I went into immediate defence mode. "Yes I do, but I was planning to do it myself."

" Oh no, can't do. Very difficult."

"Well I didn't want to spend much and I'm very experienced so it won't be a problem."

"You have sleeping bag and tent?"

"No. I'm planning on hiring them."

"Oh, very difficult," he said, "we have trip for tomorrow, you could go."

"Oh yes," I said, "how much?"

"Good price. Only forty dollars"

I laughed. "Forty dollars. I could get it cheaper than that in Sengiggi. The reason I came here was so that I could either get it very cheap or go on my own. I could get guide for forty thousand and hire the equipment and food no problem."

"Okay, I give you cheaper. Thirty dollars."

"Can we stop talking dollars please. I'm Scottish[4], we don't have dollars. How many rupiah?"

"Three hundred thousand."

---

4 Indonesians seemed to think English people were rich; they hadn't really heard of Scotland.

"Why would I want to spend that? I could go on my own. No problem. In England, er Scotland, I walk on my own all the time."

"You need guide."

"Maybe if I take longer route, but really I would like to go on my own. It's no problem. I don't have much money."

The guy was obviously now thinking on his feet (in a sitting down fashion) and I was calculating exactly what I did want from the situation. I was once again in that backpacking twilight zone of knowing that someone is giving me x amount of bullshit but not knowing the value of x. It may be vaguely possible to work out the value of x but it takes: a) an up-to-date book; b) recent first-hand reports; c) experience; d) time. I had a little bit of the third and that was it.

"Okay," he said, "tomorrow we have trip with French girl. He (sic) is going on three day trip with guide and porter. You could maybe follow guide and take porter for two hundred thousand."

This was beginning to sound interesting. It was already a lot less than the prices in Sengiggi but more than I thought a trip organised by myself would be. I carefully asked him to explain more. He gave me the details of the trip – up to the rim, down into the caldera to the lake and hot springs, back to the rim and back here – three days and two nights.

"Okay," I said, "but it still sounds a bit expensive. What are the chances of going right to the top?"

He explained that this usually took four days and three nights (which is what I had heard), however, I was 'lucky' (his words) as the French girl was doing the long trip but in three days and two nights (which would also be convenient for him as I could be a lucrative addition to this). A four day trip would wipe out the option of the Gili Islands but a shorter trip could be okay. The question was, was it possible? This peak was at an altitude of almost 4,000 metres and shortening the journey time by 30% seemed extreme, but I was interested.

I asked him to explain more and with the aid of a sketchy map he told me that we would get a Jeep at 5am to Sembalun Lawang on the other side of the mountain, walk all day to the rim, camp overnight, get up early, climb to the top, come back down, descend to the crater lake, stop at the hot springs and then climb up the other side on the second day, and then trek back to the guest house on day three. This volcano dominated the island and the idea of travelling to the far side, reaching the summit, descending 1,500 metre cliffs into the 8 kilometre-wide caldera and climbing back out again in that time sounded impossible but the guy assured me it would be okay, adding as an aside, "You will have to pay another twenty-five thousand for transport."

I now had some serious thinking to do. I was still convinced I could arrange something myself, but to be able to do all he had said in the time scale I wanted sounded pretty good. I still acted relatively unimpressed and had a quick chat with Wayan when the guy went off to do something. Wayan said he thought it was a very good price but I wasn't sure about his impartiality. The guy came back and said I needed to make a decision as he had to get a porter and food, etc. Looking back now I'm not sure why I was so uncertain but I think I was hooked on the challenge of doing it completely independently and also had an inherent suspicion of anything that might be a bit too organised or 'touristy'. I needed to think quickly as it was now approaching 4:00 and I wanted to see the stick-fighting. I told him I was going to go to my room to check my money situation and I went and weighed up all the options. It took a minute to decide that, of course, this was a fantastic opportunity to do the whole thing in a short time and I returned to do the deal. The guest house boss was out there and I confirmed a couple of points. I then suggested I paid half now and half on our return. The boss took this as an ungentlemanly slur on his professionalism so I reluctantly relented. On paying the money, he informed me that the French girl had paid 1,000,000Rp and that I should stay quiet about the price but if asked say that I paid 400,000Rp.

"Of course," I said.

I'll make my own decisions, I thought, wondering what she would make of the whole thing.

The French girl walked by at this point and I briefly said "Hi". Slim with dark hair, I'd hoped that she was going to look like Juliette Binoche in *The English Patient*, but she didn't.

I went back to my room to get some film and as I locked the door, noticed that a bemo was waiting to take me down to the stick-fighting. I had been keen to fit the waterfall in as well but it would have to wait.

As I walked to the road, Wayan sidled up to me.

"You give me money?"

I looked at him, surprised. "I'm sorry?"

"You give me money for bring you here?"

"But you were coming here anyway, you were on the bus."

"You give me money to go home."

"But why? You spoke to me. I thought you being friendly."

"You give me money?"

I was unconvinced and looked at the guest house bunch who nodded.

"You should give him small money."

I was annoyed but not annoyed enough to make a point. He'd been a nice guy and I guessed he had made the trip a bit easier; I gave him a few thousand and got into the waiting bemo wondering if I should have seen that coming and how best to measure the kindness of strangers.

Dropped in the main village, I followed the crowds along a dusty, bumpy track to I knew not where. Motorcycles raced by sounding like large, bronchial mosquitoes and there was an air of excitement. Two hundred metres along there was a traditional bamboo village in a compound and a field thronged with three to four hundred people. It was clearly the Sasak equivalent of a fête with kids running around, food stalls and families on blankets. In front of me was a large circle of men and above them older kids were hanging from trees, obviously trying to get a better look at whatever was going on. I slowly moved forward in a feeble attempt not to make myself look too conspicuous; always an easy task when you're six feet tall, white as the driven snow and carrying a camera the size of a cooking pot. I felt slightly more at ease when I spotted three other Western faces in the throng.

The circle was about five people deep and the area within it about eight metres in diameter. Dominating the centre was a man in his fifties who seemed to be the Master of Ceremonies. Casually dressed in a short-sleeved shirt and slacks, he was stirring up the crowd with tales of great achievement, occasionally resorting to the aid of an old microphone attached to a couple of trees which seemed to have grown loudspeakers. With two helpers he prowled around the ring focusing on various individuals and yelling from time to time; this would make the crowd shy away in a mixture of dramatic and actual fear. Eventually he pulled a young guy from the crowd to a loud cheer and then attempted to find another. Individuals who were pushed forward by good-humoured friends would frantically attempt to move away; at other times the MC would grab someone's arm who would struggle not to get pulled into the ring.

He finally found another contender and the two young men were prepared. They took off their shirts and place bandannas on their heads; they were then presented with a buffalo-hide shield, about 60 centimetres in diameter, and a rattan stick which looked over a metre in length (rattan is a climbing palm with tough stems). There was an excited buzz around the crowd. The MC introduced the fighters who played their parts with much bravado as the crowd let out massive whoops and cheers. The front row was made to sit down and he explained some rules he wanted obeyed to the fighters ("...clean fight lads, no spitting or hair-pulling, best of luck..."). He set them in the middle of the ring. He yelled. There was silence. One loud blast on the whistle. Complete havoc. With incredible speed and ferocity the two fighters went at each other, each attempting to land several blows on his opponent in quick succession, the blows being skillfully parried by stick and shield. They sped about the ring which moved to accommodate them as they got perilously close. Only twenty seconds on they were lashing blows in close proximity when the MC and helpers frantically started blowing whistles and dived in to break up the fight. One of the fighters jumped back smugly and was announced as the winner to whoops of delight. Everything calmed.

It was an incredible sight, heightened by the fact that I had had no inkling as to what to expect. As the process began again I tried to make sense of what was happening. I later learned that the contest was called *Peresehan* and a common occurrence amongst the Sasak people of Lombok. The MC or *Pekembar* (umpire) prowled around the ring once more, yelling from time to time and lunging far into the crowd. As he grabbed young men by the arm they pulled back with nervous looks on their faces and as others were once again encouraged or pushed forward by enthusiastic friends they fought to move back into the crowd. Eventually another two contenders were found and there was excited anticipation as they prepared. It seemed that the rules were to get a body blow between shoulders and waist as quickly as possible; the umpire deciding when this had happened or stopping the contest when he felt it had gotten too rough. As they faced up to each other the umpire moved round the ring making the front rows squat down; a loud yell and a blast on the whistle and once again there was a frantic collection of blows. The fighters whirled around, scattering spectators as they moved towards them; during one particularly frantic moment the crowd was torn apart and sent flying by the action whilst accompanied by loud blows of the whistle and intervention by the umpire – once again a winner had been found.

The whole time I was attempting to watch and get pictures of the spectacle by holding my camera high in the air in classic paparazzi style. The French girl had appeared in the crowd of onlookers and asked me to do the same with her camera as I squeezed into the crowd to get a better view. After a while, the thick clouds of cigarette smoke rising from the spectators was beginning to get a little overpowering so I moved away from the circle towards a fair-haired couple who were standing nearby. They happened to be from London and we shared a brief joke about joining in just at the moment that there was a big roar from the crowd and two stick-fighters came careering towards us in a flurry of blows, chased by a frantically-whistling umpire and a crowd of cheering locals. We dived sideways to avoid the over-exuberant thrashing and I felt a fast change in air pressure when one of the sticks flew past my face. Luckily the umpire's whistle quickly did its work and with big smiles and slaps on the back the two opponents sauntered to the ring leaving me grinning at the bewildered couple opposite.

We shared a couple of jokes and I then wandered off to take some photos without being too much of a tourist. This was almost immediately unsuccessful as I was spotted by a very large bunch of very small kids whilst trying to load a new film of black and white. They encircled me with fascinated looks on their faces as I talked them through what I was doing; I then asked them if they wanted their picture taken by beckoning with my camera. There was much excitement as I took a couple of steps back and as I raised my camera they enthusiastically charged forward, almost knocking me backwards. I tried stepping back once more but was once again charged. This amusement was repeated several times until I felt that I might have the chance of a reasonable photo. With that satisfying shutter sound I clicked and said thank you with a big smile.

I walked back across the small field to the fighting in the hope of getting some good black and white shots of the combatants and the crowd. Up to this point I had been happily snapping away mostly in colour in order to capture the complexity of greens, browns, oranges and blues of Indonesia; however, I had always loved the contrast of black and white photos and the way in which they reduced a scene to its more basic elements – this seemed a good place to try this. A friendly man in a beige short-sleeved shirt came over to talk to me who, it transpired, was a guest house owner. He asked me about my plans, which I told him, and then asked if I'd tried the local brew.

"What is it?"

"Come."

He led me to a corner of the field where they were selling the stuff. I expressed my interest in buying a bottle until I noticed that the bottles didn't have anything resembling a cork but simply had cloth pushed in the top making them look suspiciously like Molotov cocktails. At 50p per bottle I would have bought one but transportation and safety may have been difficult. I apologised and began to move away but was spotted by my guest house owner who was sitting with a number of friends quaffing this dubious concoction with very relaxed smiles on their faces. He beckoned me over asking if I'd tried it. I told him I hadn't and was offered a glassful; it was the colour of old-fashioned lemonade and I assumed was rice based. I took a polite sniff and then sip, thanking them for their hospitality; the stuff was actually quite nice. They thrust the glass back towards me stressing that I was expected to drink the whole lot. I looked around the group and realised that drinking it in one had to be the way to do it. This I duly did to murmurs of appreciation. I smiled, thanked them and walked off with the straight-line motion of a snake; I then waited a couple of minutes for my legs to arrive.

The fighting had died down and people were slowly beginning to make their way home. I sauntered back down the dusty track to the road and a bemo arrived within a few minutes to take me back to the guest house. I sat in the front with the driver and we began the upward climb; after ten minutes, rounding a corner I excitedly glimpsed a view of the peak. I asked the driver how far the guest house was and he told me ten minutes walk so I paid my money and jumped out. I had to look at this and get some photos. I was spotted by the English girl from the couple I'd spoken to at the stick fight; we had a brief chat and she asked me if she could join me up to the guest house. We slowly climbed the hill and on arriving at the guest house ordered a bite to eat and some drinks whilst chatting about our adventures so far.

It was now approaching dusk so the English girl set off down the hill and I went to sort out my room. There were a few more people milling around but I took little notice of them. I got to my door and went to take my key from my pocket – it wasn't there. I fumbled through my camera case with no luck and stood there for a while trying to work out where I could have lost it, checking pockets and looking on the floor around me in an increasingly annoyed fashion. I eventually sheepishly walked to reception to inform them of my problem and they duly found their spare keys and unlocked the door for me – my key was lying on the bed.

I had a quick wash, got changed and decided it was time for more food. A very tall girl, with dark curly hair tied in a pony tail, said "Hi" as I walked up to the covered dining area and sat myself down at a table. The French girl was at another table with three other guys, talking French. I began to jot some notes in my diary when the tall girl and a blond-haired guy in a smart, long-sleeved shirt came and sat down. The girl was German and the two of them had just arrived with the intention of climbing the mountain. A couple of the French guys joined us and we all started chatting.

I turned to the blond-haired guy.

"So are you from Germany too?"

"No, I'm from Stoke."

I looked around, slightly embarrassed, as everyone laughed at me.

"Sorry I just assumed…." I said, trying to regain some credibility. When this didn't work I changed the subject back to travelling and asked him why he was here. With no obvious accent, he told me his name was Julian and he was on a short holiday from his work as an EFL (English as a Foreign Language) teacher in Japan; he and Billa, the German girl, knew each other from there and were travelling together. It transpired that we would all be going up the volcano together. Julian and Billa had negotiated a porter for the both of them with Julian carrying some of the stuff. The French guys were also going to do the trip. I was actually quite disappointed by this as the whole thing was taking on slightly bigger proportions than I'd wanted, it concerned me that it may not be the independent adventure I had hoped for, but there was now nothing I could do about it so I let those thoughts drift to the back of my mind.

There were now seven of us merrily chatting, sometimes in French (I struggled to keep up) but usually in English (I was okay at that). The French guys were good company and as is frequently common in these situations we didn't exchange names; it's amazing how often that happens, it's almost unimportant. I mentally referred to them as the funny one (dark hair, tanned smiley face), the friendly one (dark hair, likely to be a hit with the ladies) and the serious one (brown hair and possibly the oldest of the three – late twenties, I guessed). A young Indonesian had also joined us and he and I chatted from time to time. He was most interested in the Western fascination for alcohol and explained that he chose not to drink it because of his religious belief that it clouded the mind and was harmful to health; I gently probed him on the Indonesians' great love of tobacco and its associated health risks but I think my point may have been a little too subtle and I didn't want to appear rude.

We talked about the current problems.

"Very bad," he said. "Country very poor."

"What do you think has happened?" I asked.

"Dutch and English take all our money, make us poor."

But that was a hundred years ago, I thought.

"So the government is okay, yes?" I inquired.

"Yes. Dutch and English, they take our trees, take everything, leave us poor."

But I thought it was the Indonesian government that had been decimating the rainforests over the last few decades.

"And Malaysia," he continued. "They take Kalimantan." (Malaysia and Brunei made up the top third of the island of Borneo, Indonesia controlling the bottom two-thirds, Kalimantan.)

"They are bad, yes?" I asked.

"Yes, we have *Konfrontasi* with them."

"Confrontation?"

"Yes."

I wondered about the accusations against the government of economic mismanagement, corruption and human rights violations.

"So government is okay, yes?"

"Yes."

I decided not get into a discussion about the independence of East Timor.

We rejoined the general murmur of conversation surrounding us. A mass of food and drink was ordered and I was forced to explain my lack of beer to the French by telling them of my experiences with the local firewater. We chatted away as the food slowly came. The *kentang goreng* which I had finally learnt was the word for 'potatoes fried' – or chips – took over an hour and the fried chicken (*ayam goreng*) around two; I can only assume that they had to kill and pluck the chicken first. When it arrived at the table it was a disappointing collection of fried chicken parts (including beak), lacking in meat.

I had earlier asked the guy organising the trip if he intended to give me more details of the itinerary, supplies and what I needed to take; he'd assured me he would but it was now getting late and I'd still learned nothing. Everyone else seemed quite content with this – the French particularly seemed quite happy but the guy had spent some time with them earlier in the evening with a rough map of the route and had introduced them to their guides, so I guessed they were sorted. I also later learned that they were each paying significantly more than I was – over four times as much.

I asked Julian about the plans and he told me everything seemed to be as okay as you'd except in Indonesia. As for personal kit I'd pretty much have to decide on that myself. I went to my room to sort out some stuff and was encountered by an extremely large gecko, perhaps 40 centimetres in length, sitting on the wall. With its green-grey skin, large feet and big eyes it was nevertheless quite attractive as lizards go but it got me nervously wondering what other exotic wildlife might be sharing my space so I decided to check the bathroom. I tentatively pushed open the door, edging myself in slowly, and there in front of me... was an empty bathroom. I walked in and let out an audible sigh of relief; unfortunately this disturbed the spider the size of my hand which had been sitting on the wall by my knee but which now appeared to fling itself in my direction, doubling in size on the way. I was sitting back at the table within a nanosecond to amused looks from the French; when I told them what I'd seen they tried to reassure me by saying that hopefully the gecko would eat the spider – in a head-to-head I'd have feared for the gecko.

It had gone 10pm and we had just been informed that we had to be up at 4:00 for breakfast at 4:30 and a 5:00 departure. We held a quick vote and decided that 4:30 would be plenty early enough for getting out of bed. A few more words and Billa, Julian and I wandered out onto the road, away from the lights, to look at the stars. It was a fantastically clear night with the Milky Way mistily flowing through the few constellations we could identify; the view from the top was surely going to be incredible. We retired to our rooms and with such an early start I decided it would be wise to organise my packing before going to sleep. I had paid 2,000Rp for two nights to leave my main backpack so I just had to pack the small one with the essentials.

List

Walking boots	Oranges and grapes
Two pairs of socks	Sun block – factor 20
Long trousers (jogging bottoms lost)	Penknife
Long sleeved shirt	Baseball cap
Hooded sports top	Scarf
Pair of shorts	Glasses
Towel	Sunglasses
Notepad and pen	Camera
Torch and spare batteries	Film × 2 (colour and black and white)
Passport, tickets, etc. (safer with me)	Toothbrush and toothpaste
Harmonica (we may have a campfire)	Plasters (an afterthought)

It didn't take me long to work out what I thought I needed: I wanted to travel as lightly as possible but needed to take adequate clothing; I guessed it would be cold at night but I wanted to take the bare minimum due to the weight of carrying it during the day. My final list was all I had for the next three days and two nights so I'd better get it right. I just hoped the porter had anything else I may need.

I packed up my big backpack, laid out my stuff for the morning, flicked off the light and got into bed. At this point I remembered that I hadn't seen the gecko which then got me worrying about the spider, but I tried to convince myself that maybe it hadn't actually doubled in size when it moved and maybe it was actually running away from me. Nevertheless, I got up and tentatively moved my bed a short distance from the walls, crawled back into my sleeping bag and apprehensively hid inside. A few minutes passed by and I was slowly drifting into sleep when suddenly I heard an implausibly loud whirring noise close to my head. With a rush of adrenaline I pulled the sleeping bag tightly around me as the whirring abruptly stopped and I realised it was from the wall beside me. An emphatic call then filled the darkness.

"GECK-O!"

This was casually repeated five times until it quietly faded away.

Well at least it was still alive. I banged on the wall hoping it might scuttle off and went to sleep.

This communication process with the gecko was repeated several times that night until a few hours later there was a knock at the door. It was 4:30.

Facing The Challenge
(climbing Rinjani)

The journey of a thousand miles begins with one step

I fell out of bed and opened the door. It was dark apart from the lights of the dining area where everyone was seated waiting for breakfast. It was very cold. I threw on my carefully laid out clothes and went to join them, pleased at being allowed to sleep in until this time. Everyone had already put their breakfast orders in so I wandered over to the kitchen and added mine to the list. As the coffee and pancakes began arriving we ate with very little banter.

It was 5:00 when a bemo first arrived stacked with various gear. I went to sort out the stuff in my room and then carried my backpack to reception. I sat back down with the French guys and started chatting. After a short while one of them turned to me.

"Weren't you supposed to be going with the French girl?"

"Yes, where's she got to?"

"She left a few minutes ago."

I looked at them, too tired to get stressed out by this.

"Oh well, I'm sure it's in hand."

The bemo in the forecourt was being loaded with stuff and we were all standing in anticipation. The French guys were called over and I wondered why I was still waiting, as were an impatient-looking Billa and Julian. They were all beckoned on to the bemo and I thought now was the time to find out what was happening. I collared one of the organisers.

"Shouldn't I be going with these?"

"No. You go next time," he replied in a tone of voice which was either extremely curt or a cultural/language difference.

"But I should have gone with French girl. Your boss said so."

He had a brief conversation with another guy and turned back to me.

"No. You go next time."

Thank you. Very helpful. It can be very frustrating organising trips in this part of the world as getting straight, clear answers is often impossible. At the end of the day all you can do is keep in perspective the amount you are paying and be as aware as possible of cultural differences in things like timekeeping and trade descriptions. This can be difficult when you were up at 4:30.

The French guys were observing the conversation and the friendly one beckoned to me from the back of the bemo.

"Come with us now."

I wasn't sure what to do but luckily the serious one spoke Indonesian and had a word with one of the 'organisers'. After a minute's conversation he turned to me.

"It's okay. Another bemo will be along for you three soon. We will wait at the start to make sure you arrive."

There didn't seem to be much else I could do so I relented and bid them *au revoir* – it had gone 5:30. They left. I looked at Billa.

"This is a bit poor isn't it?"

She mumbled something in agreement.

"Where's Julian?" I asked.

"Gone to sleep," she replied. He was obviously expecting a long wait.

We returned to our seats and glumly sat there reflecting on crap Indonesian organisation – it was an hour past our estimated time of departure of 5:00. I was desperately trying not to let it spoil what was supposed to be the beginning of an amazing experience.

We chatted intermittently and I eventually got round to asking her how much she'd paid. She told me 400,000Rp which coincidentally was what the owner had told me to say I had paid if asked; I didn't feel it would be politic to say that I'd paid 225,000, so I told her it was around 300,000.

It was getting lighter when Billa said she could hear a vehicle; I thought she was making it up, but shortly a bemo turned into the guest house and we were beckoned over. We jumped up and Billa shouted for Julian a number of times until he was woken from his slumbers. It was around 6:30 and we were off almost immediately, but as we descended the hill I looked at the gear sitting beside Sirip, the tall porter Julian and Billa had met the day before, and thought it didn't look like much for three people. My fears were alleviated as we got to the village and a second man got on with his own broad bamboo pole with all sorts of boxes and bags tied to it. This was to be my porter, Rana, a cheerful guy who spoke pretty good English. He told us he'd been waiting there since 4:30 but they'd forgotten to order an extra bemo. Genius. The guy I'd first haggled with at the guest house stuck his head in and apologised for the cock-up. I was too relieved to do anything other than nod my acceptance as he thrust a bottle of water at me. Finally everything was looking fine as we set off on the forty minute drive to the starting point. A few words were exchanged on the bumpy, winding journey as we made our way to the other side of the volcano but we were generally quiet due to a mixture of anticipation, tiredness and discomfort.

We finally reached the village of what I guessed was Sembalun Lawang at around 7:15 and as we left it the bemo slowed to a standstill. A collection of villagers were concentrated by the entrance to a track. The French guys were there but disappeared quickly on our arrival; they had obviously been waiting for us to check that we got there. We unloaded our gear amongst the curious locals and I wondered how I was going to relieve the burning urge I had to go to the toilet.

Sirip and Rana began to check their loads and finely balance each end of their stout bamboo poles. I took the opportunity to pull out my camera and grab a quick shot of the last minute preparations. Sirip was tall and gangly, aged around forty, with short hair and a long face. Covering his legs was a checked sarong that only just came over his knees and so accentuated his long legs which were finished with that classic hiking footwear – flip-flops. Rana was small and stocky with a darker complexion and dark curly hair – almost Australian-aboriginal in appearance. Dressed in deck shoes, tracksuit bottoms, white T-shirt and baseball cap, he possessed a stock expression which spoke the Indonesia equivalent of "I haven't eaten breakfast, the train was late again and I'm slightly concerned about the central heating" but this could easily be replaced by a cheerful smile which said "You know, Nick, you're all right and of course I'll give you a hand fixing your car; lovely day isn't it?"

Billa was behind them, correctly kitted out in walking boots, walking shorts and fleece, with her curly hair tied back. She was helping Julian, whose tall, slim frame and blond hair stood out amongst the villagers who were carefully taking notes.

Once the bamboo poles, bristling with pans, water bottles, boxes and bags were perfectly balanced, Sirip and Rana hoisted them onto their shoulders. Rana's pole was probably as long as he was tall but he held it nonchalantly across his right shoulder with one hand. With the water attached it must have been extremely heavy and I wondered what sort of supplies we would be able to get on the way; the sort of thing you would expect to check beforehand but I knew that the question would be answered with "No problem, don't worry", so I trusted in Allah's grace.

It looked as if everyone was ready to go so Julian and I scuttled up the track and found a convenient place to empty our bladders.

Billa wandered by, grinning, and we made some comment about it being a male bonding/guy thing. As Sirip and Rana began to come up the track we turned to begin our journey. We were already at an altitude of over 1,500 metres but it didn't feel particularly high. The track leading from the road was like a classic English bridle path with high hedges on either side; gently sloping fields were in the distance dominated by the mass of the volcano. I led the party with Rana behind me and said a few words about what a nice day it was and was he looking forward to the trip; he smiled and nodded and said something polite in return. I felt unsure about the rules of explorer-porter etiquette – should I be in front of him or let him lead, should we talk or does one just walk? It seemed better just to get on with it for the time being, so I stopped myself from making any further comments about the nice weather we were having and walked ahead quietly.

We reached the end of the bridle path and I stopped to let Rana point me to the right through a field of knee-length grass. I looked ahead to see if I could see the French party but to no avail. We began our trek through the grass and I let the group move on ahead as I took some photos of the scenery; a brisk march and I was back with them. As I turned to look behind me I could see our route with hills in the background and low-lying mist. I stopped once again to capture the scene. The grass was getting longer now, over waist height, and though a narrow track went through it, it wasn't easily discernible. I already felt tired but had been walking for less than an hour; my constant stopping for photos and the quick marches to catch up with the group probably didn't help. I was also getting slightly worried about the grass thrashing against my bare legs and had visions of tiny razor cuts all over them; stopping to check them, however, I could see no evidence of this. At this point Julian raised the spectre of ticks in the grass burrowing into me; this stopped me worrying about tiny razor cuts and instead I spent the next few hours periodically checking my legs for ticks – especially the ones which crawl up into the genital area.

After about an hour and a half we reached forest and followed a winding track through dense undergrowth. I shot on ahead to try to get some pictures of the group pushing through the jungle and looking like the hopeless explorers in the old Tarzan movies who get picked off one by one by the natives. We soon caught up with the French connection as we continued to weave our way through the trees and undergrowth.

As we left the forest, we entered an undulating area of long grass that was shoulder height in parts and after another half an hour we reached an open hut with the title 'Position 1'. It wasn't yet 10:00. We sat on the large covered deck and Rana handed me a packet of biscuits – a nice surprise, I thought. I also grabbed a banana and ate some oranges and grapes that I shared with Billa in exchange for some of her biscuits, which were nicer than mine – a bit like Rich Tea. I guzzled down water and asked Billa to take a photo. It was now getting hot and I took the opportunity to slap on some sunblock, factor 20, above the shoulders.

We set off again with the peak to our left. The track was still through long grass but began to involve steeper slopes both up and down. We continued for about an hour, crossing over a couple of ravines using old bridges until we reached what I assumed was 'Pos. 2' – a relatively wide wooden bridge with a large sign saying the next stop was one and a half hours. I had noticed these points on the sketchy map I had been shown the day before but without a clear scale on the map it was difficult to tell how far apart they actually were.

The walk began to get much harder and we stopped briefly under the shade of a boulder for biscuits, oranges and water. Julian decided to use this as an opportunity to climb a tree and have his photo taken. With a scarf wrapped around his head he looked utterly ridiculous and one of the French guys decided he resembled

Brian of Monty Python fame – for the rest of the day, this was to be his name. I decided to sit with shades and baseball cap beneath the boulder and have my presence recorded on film that way. We climbed a short hill, descended into a ravine and crossed an extremely narrow, rickety bridge which a couple of us took photos of in order to record its rickety-ness. More walking, another ravine and within an hour we were climbing into a gorge with a steep cliff side, sheltered, with smoke rising from various points – tea, coffee and lunch was being prepared from a collection of small fires that had been started by porters from a couple of other groups. Around a dozen people were congregated here in the throes of well-earned relaxation – we were happy to join them. Within ten minutes Rana and Sirip had caught us up and began to prepare their own areas for whatever culinary delights they had in store; I took the opportunity to grab a roll-mat from Rana, carefully messing up his carefully organised pack. I laid it out beneath the cliff and lay down with a grateful sigh – and it wasn't even midday.

It was wonderfully comfortable lying there until one of the porters decided to light a fire within a couple of metres of myself and Julian, who had sat down nearby. Smoke began funnelling its way across me and after a few minutes I announced 'bollocks, I'll have to move,' much to the amusement of the group of people who had been watching this happen and had probably put bets on as to how long I would tolerate it. I found another spot a few metres away and once again made myself comfortable.

Looking over at Rana, I could see him busily looking for firewood. I began to feel a little guilty as he had carried so much with little rest so I went over to help him. We collected several bundles of wood which we brought back to the site and he started preparing a fire. I went back to my comfy spot and before long Rana was approaching with a steaming cup of coffee and some bananas, some of which Billa decided to nick. I lay there happily relaxed, only moving to take a photo of the impressive cooking skills that were being demonstrated by the porters. After a short time, Rana was walking towards me with a massive plate of fried noodles and vegetables. I certainly hadn't been expecting cuisine of this standard. I fussily asked for some soy sauce and began guzzling. Julian and Billa's porter, Sirip, was soon plying them with goodies and I noticed that this included hot chocolate – it became my personal mission to obtain some of this but I'd play a long game if I had to. I managed most of my lunch and then lay there chatting to Julian.

I scribbled some notes to myself:

Past Sembalun Lawang at 7.15
Up track like bridle path
Turn right through long grass
Continue into forest
Out of forest grass reaches shoulders
Pos 1 = hut – peak on left
Over bridges
Pos 2 = bridge with sign 1.5 hours
Walk gets harder
Into ravine, over rickety bridge down into another ravine
Takes one hour to steep sheltered cliff – pos 3? – 10.15
Hill with windy track on right

After around an hour I was once again getting restless. It was still not yet noon. I took a couple more photos, one of a porter skinning a pineapple and one of a silhouetted tree, and wandered up the gorge and back again. Billa and Julian were also shaping to move so I took the roll-mat back to Rana, thanked him for lunch and checked it was okay to go on. He said the trail was pretty clear from here and the approximate time to the rim was, to my surprise, only around three hours; it seems we had made excellent time to our lunch stop and were likely to get to the campsite by 4:00.

Julian, Billa and I were pointed up a track leading out of the gorge and we headed straight off. There was more waist high grass but the terrain was now increasingly undulating and becoming steeper. I finished off my black and white film and switched back to colour. We had decided to move on quickly in order to gain altitude before the hot mid-afternoon sun attacked us but as we climbed higher the air began to get noticeably cooler with swirling clouds attempting to envelop the whole area.

We continued to chat through our ascent, taking short breaks every forty minutes or so. Julian shot on ahead for a while as Billa and I continued trekking steadily upwards.

From time to time we would reach outstretched ridges with long grass, scattered trees, and steep slopes either side that were bathed in clouds. Looking back I could see Rana and other parties following on behind us, the land appearing to float in a misty sea.

The dirt track was now very steep as we moved through grassland and then woodland where Billa and I caught up with Julian as we climbed up through the intermittent shade. Twenty minutes into the sparse woods we stopped for a quick break and for some reason I decided to carve my initials into a tree trunk, something I'd never done before. I pulled out my penknife and made a feeble start. Julian, who was obviously much more skilled at this kind of thing, informed me that I was doing it all wrong and took over. I completed it with his help, at which point he told me it was an act of vandalism and his brother wouldn't be impressed. The relevance of this became apparent when he informed us that in the early 1990s his brother had been one of the last protesters evicted from the road-building at Twyford Down, Newbury, and had gone to prison. Very impressive, we thought, despite our unnecessarily disparaging comments about tree huggers.

Rana caught us up with a smile and a wipe of the brow. His T-shirt was stuffed into the band of his trousers and his baseball cap was on backwards; either sheltering his neck from the sun or a statement of style. Despite the distance and height we had walked he didn't seem at all tired. He wasn't a big guy but his broad shoulders and strong, defined arms pointed to a level of strength and stamina which I couldn't even begin to aspire to.

We continued climbing – now very tired and with the hope that every ridge ahead of us was the top, too often it wasn't. Eventually, however, the edge of the rim did come into sight with a narrow path leading upwards along a ridge and through trees towards it; with clouds either side it was like the entrance to some mythical land. The ground began to flatten out and I felt that I should be able to see something of note, but still nothing. The sky around us was bleached white and either side of the ridge there was nothingness. Finally, there was the contained area of the campsite, perched on the edge of a cliff. The view, however, was non-existent. A white canvas stretched out downwards, sideways and upwards with just the edge of the cliff clearly visible – no crater, no lake, yet no anti-climax – we had made it this far and the anticipation was enough to keep the excitement simmering. We descended to the campsite where there were already a couple of tents erected by other adventurers. Rana picked a prime spot for my tent and began to sort out the gear. I sat on the ridge resting, impressed at the time we had taken – we had walked over 12 kilometres, climbing from around 1,500 to almost 3,000 metres – an estimated nine hour journey had taken six hours and we were now at well over twice the altitude of the highest peaks in the UK.

Within minutes we were being investigated by the local monkey population. Initially they were extremely wary but gradually they began to slowly venture within ten metres of the site. As soon as any of us raised our cameras, however, they were off; grey balls of fluff tumbling through the undergrowth and disappearing down onto the cliffs of the cloud-covered caldera.

The French party arrived and the skies slowly began to clear. Julian bounded up to a small, steep-sided ridge overlooking the camp for his picture to be taken – it looked very impressive so I followed suit – Indiana Langston on his way to the crater of doom.

The sun was now burning brightly but the altitude kept the temperature down. The area around the campsite had cleared of cloud and I took the opportunity to photograph the scrubby, uneven slopes punctuated by small trees and bushes; our rocky outcrop, the only flattish piece of land in sight, ending in a steep cliff that fell down into drifting whiteness.

I asked Julian to take a picture of me looking strong and proud with the cliffs and the seas of clouds behind me; instead I succumbed to everyone's amusement at my pomposity and burst out laughing. As this was happening, the clouds beneath us began to clear and there was my first glimpse of the massive caldera with the crater lake far below us looking like a sea and the towering cliffs on the other side like a far away impenetrable island. The Segara Anak (child of the sea) crater-lake, bluer than turquoise, was brushed by intermittent areas of soft whiteness but 8km away on the other side of the caldera's 800 metre high cliffs were dense piles of cloud pushing hard against the outer rim but seemingly unwilling or unable to cross it. It was like dry ice for a performance of mythical proportions. Above was clear blue sky accompanied by a few undecided strands of cirrus clouds who should have been somewhere else. I attempted to capture it all on film as best I could and wandered back towards the camp.

Rana was busy chopping firewood so I watched him for a short while and then once again took in the astonishing scene around us. Above us the ridge that led to the summit was beginning to clear and for the first time we could finally see the peak – red rock with clear blue sky on one side and clouds rushing up from the lake on the other; it really didn't look at all far. Once on the ridge that led up to it, Julian and I estimated an hour and a half; we even vaguely discussed going up there for sunset but decided to preserve our strength. Exactly how ridiculous our estimates were would become apparent. In the caldera below we could see no sign of *Gunung Baru* ('Mountain New'), the volcanic cone which had risen from the water, but we assumed that it must be to our left where the lake curved round behind the ridge. It would have to wait until tomorrow.

There was now little to do but relax. Rana had lit the fire and erected the tent so I grabbed the roll-mat and found a spot on the edge of the cliff. It was at this point that I finally got chatting properly to the French guys. They were all obviously avid photographers and were snapping anything that stayed still for long enough. The one I'd labelled friendly had a particularly annoying camera that beeped loudly as he focused it. Tall, dark hair and annoyingly good-looking, he spoke good English with a good sense of humour as he told me about some serious damage he had done to himself the previous week. Apparently, whilst experiencing Indonesian roads on a motorbike, he went to overtake a bus which then decided to overtake a car with drastic results. He was sent skidding off the road at speed and left lying in a ditch. Luckily he was seen by some passing tourists, but the damage involved losing a large amount of skin from his legs and particularly his arm. In the circumstances perhaps this could be considered lucky, but the damage looked awful. His injuries had to be uncovered so they could heal, and obviously caused a lot of discomfort. He dealt with it by shrugging his shoulders, covering his arm with a sheer sarong and having it bathed with iodine by his friends.

The funny one was the tallest of the three. Deeply-tanned and tall he was quick with a smile or an amusing comment; he seemed to enjoy everyone's company. The third, the most serious of the three, was slim with short brown hair and less gregarious than the others; as time went on I realised that this was more to do with his quieter personality than my original unwarranted and poorly judged perception of gallic reticence.

We relaxed happily on the edge of the cliff for the rest of the afternoon. Rana made me drinks and some *nasi goreng* (fried rice), which I couldn't finish and we all chatted amiably. A favourite topic of conversation was the chicken that had first appeared at the guest house as we were leaving. It was a relatively healthy, albeit scrawny thing and was now attached to a young porter who was ambling around aimlessly, carrying this creature by the legs. The chicken would cluck from time to time in a resigned, "Do you really have to wander around with me upside-down, I'm getting a headache" kind of way. This was possibly the least of its problems as the French had been told they were getting fresh chicken curry but none of us had quite believed it. The chicken continued its constitutional for about an hour until for ten minutes we didn't notice it. But then it appeared again and we began to think that maybe it was just a pet. This thought was banished twenty minutes later when the young porter ambled past clutching a piece of scrawny white flesh by a pair of legs. None of us were quite sure how to react, so we all laughed. The French got their curry later on but were distinctly unimpressed by it – the chicken had died in vain.

Approaching 6:00 and we psyched ourselves up for the sunset. I had spent the last hour lying on my stomach captivated by what had to be one of the best views in the world. The air was beginning to chill slightly and so I changed into warmer gear for the evening. We lined up and waited for the show.

On the far side of the caldera, the clouds built up in even greater ranks against the outer rim with lengthening stretches of cirrus cloud above us. As the sun sank over Bali, due west, we could see the clear outline of Gunung Agung, an impressively high volcano, which was dwarfed by this one. The sky filled with oranges, browns and pinks as the golden sun slowly disappeared into the clouds and a noticeable chill quickly set in.

I lay flat on my mat, pulled my sweatshirt hood over my head and looked up at the sky, awaiting the stars. We chatted and laughed and set challenges about who would be first to the top – would it be claimed by England, Germany or France? We also discussed the time we should start and the porters estimated a three to four hour climbing time so we should be up at 3:00.

One of the porters planted a candle amongst us with a plastic bottle to protect it from the wind. Everyone congregated around it as if it would keep us warm. As the sky darkened and it got colder, Julian and I grabbed our sleeping bags and brought them outside. Around us we could see small fires and candles. Slowly people wandered to their tents until just Julian and I were left trying to unscramble constellations. There were so many yet we could identify so few. The most obvious was Scorpio but it was partly eclipsed by a thin but very obvious belt of cloud going right across the sky. Both of us commented on this but it wasn't until later that I realised the obvious – it was the clearest view I had ever had of the Milky Way. We chatted for a while until Billa yelled from her tent.

"Could you two stop talking so loud!"

"Yeah, bloody rosbif," added one of the French. We apologised and Julian decided to make his way to bed.

I still felt I had to make the most of such a beautiful night. I took my diary from my tent and lay outside writing for about twenty minutes; as my arm tired I turned over to look at the smooth black sky, awash with flecks of bright silver; I reluctantly packed up my stuff and went to my tent. I took off my sweatshirt in order to feel the benefit the next morning and crawled into my sleeping bag in socks, trousers and a shirt. It was 8:00.

I awoke with a start. I was sure people were stirring and in the blackness all I could do was visualise the French setting off and claiming the peak for themselves. I frantically fumbled around for my torch, scattering my few belongings around the tent – where was the fucking thing? Finally I found it under the towel I was using as a pillow and turned it on to check the time – it was 9:30 – I'd been asleep for an hour and a half. I cursed myself quietly and went back to sleep.

The rest of the night was miserable. I awoke at least every hour, freezing cold and would attempt to change position to make myself warmer but with little success. Eventually there was movement outside.

"Where are you England?"

It was 3:00 and time to move.

I put on my boots, sweatshirt, baseball cap and scarf and crawled out into the freezing night with my small backpack containing a few supplies. Water was already being boiled and before long I had a hot coffee in my hands; looking back this probably made all the difference.

Scaling Heights
(attempting the summit)

If you can force your heart and nerve and sinew
To serve your turn long after they are gone

The normal advice on climbing to arrive at the summit for sunrise was to be up at 2:00 but it was 3:30 as we left the site with more jokes about who would claim the mountain. Around fifteen porters and trekkers snaked their way out of the campsite; two guides at the front and myself somewhere in the middle of the group.

The night was pure, calm and light enough for me to dispose of my torch after a short while; a number of people still hung on to theirs which made it difficult for my night vision to adjust. We scrambled up and over rocks and then reached a long steep series of narrow gullies which, I imagined, would gush with water during the rainy season. These were now thick with dust and dirt, often many centimetres deep, which would slip and disappear beneath our feet. As I made my way I tried to pull myself up using the branches of spindly bushes and trees, trying to avoid scratches and tears to my hands and clothes. The gullies got steeper and often I would be pulling myself almost vertically with no grip, just dirt and dust underfoot. The constant slipping began to wear at the leg muscles and we all quickly began to tire. We continued our ascent and a couple of times I slipped, once sinking one arm deep into the dirt as it slipped below me whilst my other arm frantically tried to grab a tree root to pull myself up and thorns dug into my hand. After around about half an hour the terrain became steeper and we stopped for a brief rest. Julian, Billa and I were keen to carry on and as the guides continued I found myself leading the pack. When we had started I had felt no real urge to race to the top but I now felt motivated by the position I was in. We continued our climb at a good rate and the pack began to stretch itself out.

As we left the dirt gullies and came to steep rocky ground we could see torch lights stretched out below us. The guides didn't seem overly confident in their route but eventually gestured in a vague direction and we carried on. As they slowed behind us, three or four of us continued upwards with, I think, Billa at the front. A few minutes went by and I heard calling from below which I thought was someone saying we had gone the wrong way, but individually we all seemed to have a strong sense of purpose now and simply wanted to press on. The climb was steep but I was now moving reasonably well. I could see the ridge that led to the top straight ahead of me and believed that to be the main goal; the rest of the climb would be easy going.

It was completely silent as we clambered upwards. I could feel myself tiring and began to stop more and more often. Billa and one of the French guys had stretched out ahead whilst Julian and I became progressively distanced as I began to rest more frequently. I was slightly pissed off that they were carrying on at this rate but it was really my annoyance at my own inability to keep up. Far below me, however, I could see pools of light; we were a long way ahead of the following pack. I hadn't really cared about this before but now I liked the idea of being one of the first up there. I took a deep breath and continued the climb. The ridge came closer and as I reached it I could see the silhouette of the cliffs opposite, the deep darkness of the caldera, the route we had taken stretching below me, and the well-defined ridge leading to the summit. The sky was clear and Orion lay brightly just above the peak.

Julian was there, resting; the others had gone on ahead. We sat and had a quick drink, acknowledging our poor estimate of the time this leg would take but estimating another hour to the top – it had gone 4:30.

The ridge was gently sloping and we set off at a quick pace. Julian seemed absolutely fine but I had felt very tired earlier; this part of the rim, however, was easier and with concentration I was happy to march at a quick rate. We continued on for a while and though I don't know how it happened, I found myself walking on my own. I guessed Julian was not too far behind me but I had now got into a steady rhythm. I was feeling very tired from the exertions of yesterday's walk and the current climb; the only way I could deal with this was by repeatedly counting my steps 1, 2, 3, 4, and trying to keep them steady and slow. I realised that I'd been trying to move too fast and that steady slow steps could be more effective. I was barely raising my legs as I trudged ever upwards along the narrow rocky path. From time to time I would look up from my efforts and try to appreciate where I was; this would give rise to feelings of real satisfaction and at one particular point I gave myself a round of applause. The ridge now stretched down behind me, steep on the side I had climbed and almost vertical down into the crater; in front of me was the steep ascent up to the summit and to my left there were valleys and plains leading out to the sea.

I continued on my own at my own pace and had no sense of anybody around me. At one point the ridge narrowed and I walked with a sheer cliff into the caldera, 1,200 metres below, right beside me. I still had no need for my torch and the darkness meant that I had little sense of height – I was glad of that. I had been moving at a reasonable pace and began to make out the outline of people up ahead; after a few minutes there was a call.

"Hello England!"

It was one of the French guys (it didn't register which one) and with him was the voice of Billa.

"So you caught up with us."

"Yeah. I've been counting my way up and don't feel too bad now. I was exhausted earlier," I said as I tried to make out their features in the darkness.

"Where's Julian?"

"I don't know. We walked together for a while but I got a steady pace going and didn't really want to slow down."

We had some water and then moved off together. The ridge began to get much steeper and the terrain more difficult. We slipped more and more frequently and eventually began to stretch out. The French guy was ahead of me and Billa was falling further behind. Soon it was just me and the French guy struggling upwards. We were now at around 3,500 metres, the ridge was getting steeper and we had reached the part of the ascent that previous climbers had spoken about. It was a 30 to 45 degree slope of scree – volcanic rock of all sizes, dusty and deep, which was formed, I guessed, by molten lava solidifying in mid-air and then broken down by rain erosion. There was no track to follow, just a constantly moving stream of gravel beneath us. It was also now noticeably colder and my baseball cap was tight to my head with the hood over it.

We moved slowly with sudden surges forward in an attempt to push ourselves up the slope – it was the equivalent of walking up a down escalator made of moving stones. There was nothing to hold on to except, from time to time, an occasional outcrop of rock or large boulder that we would closely circumnavigate in an attempt to find a firmer footing. At other times I moved closer to the cliff edge where the scree was less extreme. This took me around the right hand side of an outcrop of rock and I was now on the side of the ridge which dropped, a couple of metres away from me, straight down into the bottom of the caldera. I could feel the conveyor belt of stones pulling me down the short slope towards the 1,400 metre drop and as I attempted to quickly and carefully scramble away from the extreme edge of the ridge my feet slipped from under me.

There was nothing firm to hold but I frantically dug my hands into the gravel in order to stop the slide and, whilst trying to get a foothold, managed slowly to move myself away from the edge as stones disappeared behind me into the deep darkness. With an adrenaline-fuelled grin I muttered, "Close one" and found safer ground just behind the French guy who was still making his steady progress. He seemed to slow down for me but the scree was now even deeper and steeper and I was having to stop every couple of minutes or so. I could hear increased encouragement coming from the front but this only served to prove something I'd always known but which had never been tested to this extent – I dislike encouragement – if I can't motivate myself then it's pointless anyone else trying.

From time to time the French guy waited for me and asked me how I was getting on but this made me feel more and more frustrated at my inability to keep up. He spoke of both of us getting there together and I suggested waiting for Billa near the summit (she was now nowhere to be seen) but I was clearly a lot more tired than him and he eventually got the message to surge on ahead. Once again I was on my own.

I continued struggling upwards; resting every few minutes and, where possible, trying to find a firm foothold. Earlier, Julian had mentioned walking with your feet as flat as possible to the ground on this kind of terrain and this seemed to be relatively successful. Eventually my slow steady pace led me to an area where the ground levelled slightly and for the first time in what seemed like hours I stood up straight, pulled my hood off and let out an audible and satisfied "Yes". The mountain immediately punished my arrogance by whipping the cap off my head and flinging it thirty metres down the ridge.

"Oh fuck," I murmured to myself, quickly debating the merits of chasing after it. Stupidly I did, following it down to the extreme cliff edge and tentatively crawling towards it. The gravel slipped below me and I wondered whether a baseball cap was worth the drop into the crater lake. I carefully reached out, hoping that the precarious-looking ground was stronger than it seemed. It held as I happily grabbed the cap, crawled back from the edge and slowly retraced my steps back up. We'd been through a lot together.

The ground steepened once again. The wind seemed to be increasing in strength and each time I stopped I quickly felt it cutting through my clothes. I had little idea as to how cold it was but at 5 degrees Celsius and a wind speed of 50 kilometres per hour, the wind chill would have been around -20 degrees. Altitude Sickness or Acute Mountain Sickness was something else to which I had given little thought but I later learned that the symptoms of headache and nausea can kick in at 2,500 metres due to the change in oxygen levels, especially if the individual has ascended from lower altitudes too quickly; 18 hours earlier I'd been at sea level but luckily I felt fine, albeit breathless.

I continued struggling upwards, resting briefly every couple of minutes. The blasting wind and the crunch of the scree beneath my feet was like silence; I felt the complete solitude of being in such an inhospitable place – it was exhilarating. Either side of me the steep slopes fell into darkness and the ridge stretched out ahead, seemingly endless.

Up ahead I could see some bodies cowering by a rock; I couldn't work out who it could be but as I approached I realised it was a couple of guys from a different group who I guessed had camped slightly further up the volcano. I muttered a greeting which they barely acknowledged and as I approached they decided to continue their climb just ahead of me. At that point I found this particularly annoying as it made me less able to concentrate. Added to that was the bright pair of trousers one of them was wearing which I found particularly offensive at that moment in time. I muttered "Twat" quietly to myself.

I followed them for around twenty minutes, not having the energy to burst past, but at a point where they slowed slightly I took a route around them and concentrated hard in trying to pull away. Once again I was on my own; despite the clear night, I couldn't see anybody either ahead of me or behind.

The narrow ridge leading up to the summit stretched towards Orion who was lying on his side ahead of me, fantastically bright and a clear guide. As I gained in altitude and the direction of the rim curved in a more southerly direction, the wind became increasingly fierce, striking the unprotected east side of the rim and gusting over the top. The force was relentless and I wondered how hard it would have to be to send me flying into the crater lake, 1,500 metres below me. My legs were now screaming. Every time I tried to gain a foothold I slipped back and felt huge amounts of energy draining away. The ridge was ever steeper now and even areas of harder rock were giving way beneath my feet; scrambling for handholds was pointless. I was taking three or four steps and then stopping each time, perhaps gaining a metre. At this point the only thing I could do was yell at myself, something I would normally have thought was ridiculous but at that moment seemed the only constructive thing I could manage.

"For fuck's sake, come on!" I shouted at the top of my voice and continued something similar for the next ten minutes or so as I struggled slowly upwards.

I thought of the Ranulph Fiennes book I had recently read and wryly thought how pathetic this was compared to a 90 day crossing of Antarctica. I also thought, however, that despite how I was feeling there was no way I wasn't going to succeed.

I moved through an area where narrow channels had been cut into the rock by rain erosion and the ground was deep with fine gravel; I pulled myself up as best I could. I decided to take a brief rest and took off my backpack to get some water. The wind, perhaps 50 to 70 kilometres per hour, blasted around my ears and tore through my clothes, unrelenting. Looking down the ridge I thought I could make out some figures approaching who I assumed were the guys I had encountered earlier. I continued on, occasionally looking behind me to see if they were gaining. I now desperately wanted to be one of the first to the top.

The sky seemed to be lightening and I looked to my wrist for the time. I couldn't see my watch and rather oddly I checked the whole of my left arm to see if it had moved – it definitely wasn't there. Bollocks, I thought. It must have disappeared earlier when I was scrabbling around, my best guess was when I slipped just after leaving camp or when I stopped my slide on the ridge. I took a guess at 5:00 to 5.30 and seriously began to wonder if I would make it for sunrise. The distance wasn't that great but I was barely travelling at 2 metres per minute. The terrain was now extremely steep, the gravel gave less grip and firmer areas would break away beneath my feet and in my hands. It was now a question of taking three steps forward and slipping back two. I could see a point, perhaps fifty metres ahead, where the ground looked as if it may get firmer but at that time it could have been fifty kilometres away – it appeared completely unachievable.

I began to wonder if I would make it, but paradoxically thought that there was no way I wouldn't; I couldn't imagine allowing myself to stop climbing, too exhausted to move and then turn round and go back down – it wasn't an option. I desperately scrambled upwards but there was no grip at all. The only real way was quick bursts of energy but this had all but disappeared; I couldn't even stop to rest as I would just start sliding downwards whenever I paused. It was important to stay vaguely within the dusty gullies otherwise a slide could cause a fall down either side of the ridge, both of which were now fatally steep. I looked down the slope from time to time and could definitely see someone; however, their progress was as slow as mine so I tried to concentrate on my own struggle. The wind was now a constant roar and I attempted to angle my body so that it would perhaps push me slightly upwards.

Three quarters of the way up this section I encountered the worst part so far – a 45 degree slope with no grip and very deep scree. It was perhaps only a twenty metre climb to a small outcrop of rock to the right but with every step my legs screamed at me and with every rest I would slip back down. I tried using my hands but this made little difference so I scrambled as best I could and paused for as long as I was able to until the ground would start moving again. The last seven or eight metres would involve a big push but as I launched upwards there was no grip and I slipped back down, stones racing away down the slope. I tried once more and as the ground disappeared below me I got closer to the rocks; I desperately reached out. At first they disintegrated in my hands but eventually I pulled myself up and was able to angle my body against them and sit down without slipping. I took off my backpack and pulled out water and biscuits. Looking down I could see someone approaching and from the outline seemed it could be Billa. I called out and she confirmed my guess, this was great news. It seemed to take a lifetime for her to reach me; eventually she was within five metres but as she tried to push forward she slipped onto her stomach and slid a long way down. I couldn't even try to help her as I was in no position to hang on to anything. She tried again. Another scramble upwards and with a hand on my wrist she made it. We exchanged words and shared my water and biscuits. We could have sat there for ages but the wind was hitting us full on, loud and bitter. We began to get very cold – it was time to move.

Having two of us really seemed to help. We were both exhausted, but most importantly we had similar levels of fatigue. This meant that we both appreciated the regular breaks and were happy with the pace. We pushed on and came across a water bottle, which we assumed had been left by the French guy. With nervous smiles we presumed he hadn't disappeared off the edge.

The whole of the eastern sky to our left was now beginning to get light as we trudged and scrambled higher. In front of us we could see the top of the ridge that hopefully led to a short walk to the summit. As we approached we could see our route go to the right of a cliff face about six metres in height. This now seemed the main goal and with a burst of energy we thrust ourselves up the unforgiving slope to where the ground began finally to level off. We flung ourselves beneath the cliff with a great degree of happiness and relief; we guessed at perhaps another fifteen minutes to the summit but desperately needed to rest. Grateful to be sheltered from the wind, we feasted on biscuits and water.

After about five minutes we decided to finish the journey; we rounded the cliff face but as we approached the slope leading up from it we realised where we were.

I let out a yell.

"Monsieur le France!"

"England!!"

We were here.

The French guy (it was the funny one) was lying on his stomach facing east but rose to greet us as we bounded forwards, embraced and cheered. The world stretched out around us, a misty ocean of darkness. Across the eastern sky lay a thin golden band and above it the sky was turning a deep blue, causing the stars to slowly fade. Behind us the rim fell away steeply into darkness on three sides and night was still hiding in the depths of the caldera. To the west I could make out the faint outline of Bali, still waiting for the first sight of dawn.

This was where I wanted to be.

I walked around the rocky, uncomfortable summit. The ridge ended abruptly here at 3,726 metres (12,224 feet) with a sheer drop onto what looked like jagged rocks. On either side was darkness – the outer rim on one side and the caldera floor 1,700 metres below us on the other. It was an area big enough for around eight people to lie down and I tried to find somewhere to rest; however, the problem with summits is lack of shelter – it was utterly freezing and the wind was vicious. I found an area by a rock where I could lie down and pulled the last remaining item of thermal clothing out of my backpack – my towel. I wrapped it around my shoulders, basking in the warmth of the flappy object with holes in it.

We chatted about the struggle as we waited for the sun to appear and the French guy told us he had left the water we found as he couldn't be bothered to carry it any further. At our first glimpse of the sun I pulled out my camera to capture the moment. The bloody thing froze on me, just like at Bromo. The French guy's did the same. We both tried to warm them by putting them underneath our clothes but as I'd had little luck last time, I knew I was facing a losing battle and hoped that someone else might be able to help me out. As we faced the east we glimpsed someone approaching; and there was Julian. We let out a cheer as he climbed towards us – he'd made it just in time and the four of us were the first to the top.

We watched the sun rise, the wind beating into our faces, and when we realised Julian's camera was the only one that would work, the French guy, Billa and I sat together for a group photo – we would have stood but it was too cold and my towel kept flapping in an undignified fashion.

As the sun gained in height I suddenly noticed a fantastic effect to the west – a massive dark triangle had formed on the clouds below us. It was a vast shadow cast by the sun on our mountain; a shadow that came to a point where the distant horizon merged with the sky in bands of indigo, pink, orange and blue – it was an incredible sight. The summit itself, however, was still in darkness apart the glowing red daggers that the sun had thrown onto rocks as its rays were pushed through tiny gaps in the uneven ridge.

I was still utterly freezing but as bright sunlight hit the edges of the caldera and lit up the distant sea I asked Julian to take a picture of me standing on the summit and this he kindly did. The next thing we knew we were being invaded by the rest of the French contingent – they'd all made it. The French guy had joked about having champagne and saucisson – the fantastic thing was that he wasn't joking and he pulled it out of his small backpack. We stared at him in disbelief and then watched in anticipation as he attempted to launch the cork over the cliff – it travelled about a metre and we let out a cheer. As we shared the champagne, he cut slices of saucisson and we munched and drank happily. The world awoke around us. This was a wonderful place.

Above, in order: Nick, Manu and Billa
Top of facing page: Segara Anak and Gunung Baru
Below: Nick on the summit of Rinjani
Bottom of facing page: Nick on the rim

Above: The Rinjani caldera
Top of facing page, in order: Julian, Billa and Nick
Below: Travelling companions

Right: Sunset over Bali

Pictures above: Jalan Malioboro
Bottom of facing page: Jogya people
Below: A view of Sengiggi

A Very Long Day
(peaks to troughs to peaks)

Whatever you survive is good for you

We stayed on the summit for another twenty minutes or so but as it wasn't getting any warmer we decided to make our way down. We passed a couple of people at the point where Billa and I had rested earlier and then began the steep slide downwards.

Billa and Julian were obviously keen to descend at quite a fast rate. I decided to stay with the French contingent, who were moving at a slightly slower pace and stopping periodically to take photos. In my case this was a complete waste of time as my camera was still uninterested until, that is, I removed the frozen battery and it became happy to do its job, but only at a default rate of 1/1,000 of a second – not great for anything involving shade.

We tentatively felt for footholds. The descent was ridiculously steep and the grey scree unforgiving of any mistake; all I could wonder was how on earth anybody could make it up here, yet several of us did.

From where we were, the rim curved downwards in a north-westerly direction with countryside far below stretching out to the sea. To the left of me was the deep caldera with the lake and the large perfectly-formed cone, Gunung Baru, sitting in the middle, lava flows stretching into the water from the 1966 and 1994 eruptions. From our vantage point it looked tiny but that was because we were around 1,500 metres above the lake with sheer cliffs down to it. The route along the ridge we had followed varied from around one to twenty metres in width. At times there were smooth slopes running away from it, at other times sheer drops; even a fall on the slopes, however, could start a fall from which it would be difficult to recover. This was something I observed from time to time when a large rock would be dislodged and start its inexorable journey to the lake below; similar to movie scenes where just before a minor character dies on a mountain you have the picture and sounds of the rocks falling from beneath them. As we slid down the section of gravel, which I'd found such hard-going, I was amazed at how we'd managed it. With each step we descended sliding at least two or three metres. From time to time we would pretend to ski but most of the time it was a case of just letting our steps slide beneath us. My boots travelled deep into the dusty scree and whenever we stopped I emptied a handful of small stones from them. This reminded me to pick up a couple of rocks to keep as a memento and I looked with interest at the solidified, dark-grey lava speckled with tiny air pockets.

I was lagging behind the French party now, trying to appreciate the view and capture it on film with my poorly-performing camera. The new cone was now an awe-inspiring sight – too perfect to be real and so small from our vantage point. A crisp black shadow covered half of the browny-red lava flows and the crescent shaped lake, turquoise in the early morning sun, was a clear blast of colour against this and the steep brown cliffs opposite which were dotted with flecks of green. As the worst of the scree sections finished, I turned to look at the small specks of individuals descending behind me, dust flying behind them, and the rocky cliff dropping away into the depths of the caldera. In front of me the French were making their way along the ridge, bleached with sunlight on one side and deep in shadow on the other. Gradually the blackness of the cliff edge was eaten into by the harsh rays of the sun and rocks were turned into bright islands casting even darker shadows.

The ridge began to level out and there was a more discernible path that went right along the edge of the rim – this was where Julian and I had walked on a crisp night which seemed like weeks ago. It was rocky and uneven and the constant downward steps reminded my legs of how much pain they'd been in earlier. One of the French guys told me to hurry along as I lagged behind taking everything in, so I caught up with them as we left the ridge and started the descent through the wooded slopes leading back to the camp. We followed the narrow, dirty, dusty gullies, sliding downwards, the dirt sometimes coming over our boots. A couple of times we were able to slide six or seven metres downwards, the dirt rushing underneath; at other times we weren't so clever and landed on our arses – but always in good humour. We eventually saw the camp below us and I led the group along a route that to my trained eye was obviously the quickest – until we reached a three metre drop. I decided to leap downwards and cushion the fall with my back – effective but slightly painful. The rest decided to follow the nice clear path that brought them out by the camp slightly in front of me. Billa and Julian were there, grinning, and Rana had already cooked breakfast – pancakes and coffee – you couldn't ask for more – an American diner at 3,000 metres.

We talked of our adventures and enjoyed the phenomenal view of the crater and the lake – sometimes bathed in cloud and sometimes crystal clear. The steep slopes of the rim to our right were covered in trees and bushes that disappeared into a deep sea of whiteness. Our simian friends made increasingly frequent appearances, edging ever closer in an attempt to find out what kind of monkey wore clothes instead of fur.

It was approaching 9:00 and packing was in progress for the descent to the lake. I attempted to clean myself up with a small amount of bottled water and vigorous shaking of my shirt; I also changed into my other pair of socks. We may have achieved the peak but now we had to get back – two days to go.

Rana waited patiently for me and when I'd finished with the tent he quickly packed it and said he was going to go on ahead. Billa and Julian also set off but I decided to wait for the French contingent. It was only now that I really started to get to know them and, finally, their names. I hadn't even really known which of them I'd been walking with earlier until we were on the top and it was light. His name was Emmanuel, or Manu as he was called – pretty much the clown of the group, friendly with a good sense of humour, tall and broad, open and honest. Didier was the friendly one who'd had the motorbike accident and whose camera kept beeping, Olivier was the grown-up organising the group and the girl's name was Marina.

We left the camp following the path we'd taken up to it the previous day and soon we were by a track which would take us 900 metres lower to the lake by lunchtime. There were apparently two gateways into the crater – these were known as Plawangan 1 and 2 – this was number two and we would have to make it to number one by this evening – a steep climb down and another one back up the other side.

Most of the caldera was sheer-sided but at the point where we were entering there was a defined, steep path snaking downwards through the scrubby grass, small trees and bushes. At some points there was even fencing guiding us, but in reality the route was less of a path and more of a scramble down over rubble and occasional drops where the path had fallen away.

We were in bright sunshine as we left but below us there were clouds washing around the steep slopes. I walked behind Didier much of the way, a blue sarong tied around his head and covering his damaged left arm. We chatted and took photos; at least I took one to his every five. He told me that in the two to three weeks he had been here he'd taken over twenty rolls of film; I believed him.

We jumped downwards from rock to rock, the constant jarring reminding my legs how tired they were. After nearly two hours of steep descent, the ground had levelled enough to allow the path to follow a more direct route and we stopped for fifteen minutes in the hot sun for water and biscuits. We fought playfully over a couple of comfy-looking rocks and then sat with thick wiry grass on both sides and the steep cloud-washed cliffs behind us.

We continued downwards. I could see small punctuations of individuals on the slopes below me and I turned to look at several porters carrying their loads down the steep path we had just negotiated. My legs were desperately asking for a slope to walk up instead of down and eventually, following a long trek along a route which went steadily downwards and along the caldera, we reached terrain which had been affected by rain erosion where we had to traverse or circumnavigate several gullies of differing sizes. At one point there was evidence of a waterfall above us and a steep gully heading down to the lake; it seemed like a quick route but was probably virtually impossible to walk down. We climbed out of here and were soon walking down a rolling alpine-like area, towards woods with the lake behind.

The area we arrived at was obviously a major site for those visiting the volcano. There were a couple of covered areas and around twenty people were congregated there. My initial feeling was that it was a bloody mess with litter everywhere. I had read that litter was now being regarded as a major problem in Indonesia; the culture of discarding rubbish where one pleased was many times worse than in Western nations. I have heard it said that as Indonesia is a developing nation they cannot be expected to attach the same importance to issues such as litter but that is patronising in the extreme; I certainly don't believe the people of somewhere like Ubud or Yogyakarta would agree. As for the claim that tourism causes many of the problems, this may be anecdotal and simplistic but it was the Indonesian trekkers to the volcano that were dumping their rubbish where they sat, not the Westerners.

What did Rana do with our litter? I have no idea. I didn't ask and felt hypocritical afterwards; I carried mine though.

I walked down to 'the child of the sea', hoping to freshen up. In front of me, across the water, was Gunung Baru, around 300 metres in height and perhaps 500 metres in diameter, grey in colour and looking like a mountain of gravel with a flat top. Its size had been increased by the 1994 eruptions that had sent pyroclastic ash and rocks 600 metres into the air and caused the lava flows I had seen from the rim; ash clouds had been caught by satellite as high as 10,000 metres. Then in November of that year there had been a lahar, a volcanic mud slide, which had swept down one of the rivers flowing from Rinjani and killed thirty people who were collecting water.

Today there was silence apart from the lake moving gently against the shore. It seemed incredible that what looked like a mill pond was around 250 metres deep. Small areas of wispy cloud moved lazily across and occasionally tired gusts of wind rippled the surface. The sun was hot. It was 1:00.

On the edge of the empty shore, several vertical sticks were sitting in the shallows with struggling fish joined to them by a line – was catching a fish really that easy? I took off my boots, dust-caked socks and grubby shirt and ambled into the cool water. It was nice but didn't have a clear or fresh feeling to it; this wasn't helped by the number of flies buzzing around me. I left the water to rest on a log, the sun was extremely hot so I wrapped my towel over my head and shoulders and sat in quiet reflection. My back felt slightly burnt and I guessed that this was from sitting on the rim yesterday afternoon and the ten minutes I'd been standing here. I looked up at Baru and wondered how hard it would be to climb.

Didier and Manu came over to ask if I would come to the hot springs with them. I declined as I felt hungry and believed that Rana had started cooking; I thought I'd go after eating. I mooched back to Rana, who had made me a coffee, and sat resting – apart from periodic convulsions when a fly landed on me. The temperature varied continuously between midday heat and brisk chills as cloud rushed through the woods driven by chill winds.

Fried rice with vegetables was soon presented to me, carefully decorated with a fried egg on top. I was now getting sick of fried rice and noodles, and as for eggs... I ate what I could and carefully hid the rest so as not to hurt Rana's feelings – his cooking was great, my fussy nature slightly less so.

Julian and Billa returned from their sojourn to the hot springs – nice but a bit grubby they said – and I was treated to a cup of their hot chocolate – result. We chatted for a while but it was now after 2:00 and we would have to depart by 3:00. I felt that a trip to the springs was mandatory so I got directions from Rana and set off, every step a chore. It was now that I realised how exhausted I was and I wondered if this ten minute walk would use up valuable energy. My feet and legs hurt and before long I would have to climb out of this crater.

A track led me round to my first glimpse of the springs; a series of pools running away from the lake, sheltered by seven metre high cliffs. The area from where the water emanated into the first pool was the size of a five a side football pitch and inhabited by a small number of locals who had erected shelters for themselves and family. It did indeed look grubby but this wasn't helped by the nature of the place itself: sulphur deposits were on all the rocks, yellowy-greeny-white stains which were also dangerously slippy if you weren't extremely careful. I made my way to one of the pools feeling a little self-conscious as the only Westerner there. The water was flowing quickly down from one pool into another and steam was rising from it. I tentatively placed my hand in but it was the heat of very hot tap water; the pool below it seemed a little cooler but really much too hot to place any body part in. I took off my boots, socks and shirt and made an attempt to wash off two days of dirt with shallow handfuls of water; instead I managed an artistic smudging effect all over my body. A couple of Dutch guys appeared and tried to do the same thing with similar results. One of them crossed to the other side of the pool with the aid of some smooth sulphur-coated rocks. I watched with trepidation, wondering what water of this temperature would do to him if he slipped; thankfully he made it safely.

Cold winds were now gusting over the waters as clouds rushed through the woods. The mix of hot steam and icy wind was strange and I wondered about the particular characteristics of a volcanic crater that caused this strange weather.

I had been there for around fifteen minutes and knew I had to be getting back so I retraced my steps and left the springs; over my right shoulder I noticed that they continued into the near distance and wondered if the temperature down there was more appropriate for swimming. I had neither the time nor the energy to explore and returned to the camp.

Packing was in full effect and the sun was once again beating down. I found myself a quiet spot by a rock near the lake and pulled my plasters from my backpack. My feet were beginning to hurt and I wanted to give them as much protection as possible. I then covered the exposed parts of my body with sun-cream, carefully watched by a couple of Indonesian kids who found this process utterly fascinating; finally I was ready to go. We followed a track which led us right along the water's edge and I was informed by my French friends how fantastic it was swimming in the hot springs; either this lot were made of asbestos or I'd been in the wrong place. Eventually we lost sight of Baru and were guided up a track that led away from the lake, through the woods and up to Plawangan one.

We trekked upwards through long grass and trees. I turned from time to time to look at the mist-shrouded lake behind us. The ground steepened but as we rose higher the view below us became more and more impressive and eventually we were able to see Gunung Baru rising above the mist. I took a photo, desperately wanting it to clear, and as we climbed higher I was finally able to get a magnificent view of the cone, backed by massive cliffs, mist lapping at its base and our porters following the track up to where I stood. To my left I could see the long, narrow ridge leading up to the 3,726 metre summit we had climbed only that morning; once again it didn't look that far, though it did look excessively steep, and I tried to imagine something that would give this place a sense of scale – New York's Empire State Building (381 metres) or the UK's highest peak, Ben Nevis (1,344m). It was a fruitless task and I spent some time wondering what a 1,700 metre fall down a cliff felt like and at what point it stopped hurting.

I was now walking with Julian, continuously chatting but feeling utterly exhausted. The track was mainly through woods and generally steep. The sun was hot but thankfully the trees took some of the heat away. We stopped regularly for water breaks and I was extremely grateful to rest my legs each time, especially when Julian had to shoot into the woods for a long toilet break. The track continued to steepen, often requiring real effort to push upwards. After around two and a half hours of unrelenting ascent, we were within sight of the edge of the caldera; at this point a narrow path clung precariously to the side of the cliff, gradually forcing its way upwards. We passed the site of a massive rock fall and began to watch our footing with care. I could see the French contingent ahead of us and took a photo of them, dwarfed by the cliff towering by their right shoulders – they were like explorers climbing the hidden path to The Lost World. An hour previously I had been exhausted but with such an impressive end in sight it made it easier to move. I wouldn't have been overly shocked if a pterodactyl had come swooping over the cliff and my imagination started planning a response to such a situation.

I was now just 70 metres below the rim but due to the steepness of the path it was hard work; I slowed down, both to rest and also to take in everything around me. I could hear voices at the cliff edge above me, and realising I had missed the route upwards, trekked back and climbed up out of the caldera. I had made it.

This was Plawangan 1, the main gateway in and out of Rinjani. It sat 600 metres above the caldera floor and we had made it in around two hours; not a bad effort after this morning's climb to the peak and the long descent to the lake. P1 was the most popular spot for trekkers as it was the easiest way to see the caldera and could be done in an overnight trip; there were over a dozen tents scattered around on any flat piece of ground they could find. The group immediately got into a debate about where we would camp for the night. It had gone 5:00 and we needed to decide quickly as this area was patently too busy to accommodate four more tents. We wanted to be on the edge of the rim so as to take in both the sunset, which would happen behind us in just over an hour, but also the sunrise over the caldera tomorrow morning. This was going to prove difficult as Rana informed me that the next decent site was a ten minute walk from here and on the north-west slopes which meant we could see the sunset but not the sunrise. Some of our party weren't happy about this and I could feel myself getting grumpy at their inability to come to a decision. Too many cooks, or as Rana muttered to me, "*Biduk satu nahkoda dua*" – one boat, two captains.

As far as I could see, we had little choice and I also pointed out that there was a strong likelihood that we'd be too tired to get up early anyway, but if we did want to we could always trek back up to this spot. I checked with Rana that the spot was on the route back to the village and when he confirmed this I told him we should start walking. The rest of the group followed us around five minutes behind and we descended the rocky slopes down to a flatter grassy area a few hundred metres down from the rim. It took us around fifteen minutes to get there and I was a little worried that the rest of the group would feel it was too far, but when they caught up with me they seemed relatively happy and it certainly offered us spectacular views of the cloud-covered land below us. It was at this point that I realised that in my exhaustion of reaching P1, I had virtually ignored the magnificent view of the caldera and had failed to take any photographs. I shared this oversight with Billa and Julian and told them I was going back for around an hour but would be at camp just after sunset. It was around 5:30 and I wanted to get some good shots while the sun still had some height.

The trek back up to P1 really hurt but as I reached the campsite I began to take in the breathtaking views. I ran up a steep slope just to the right of the gateway where two tents were perched and in front of me was the vast caldera with its sheer cliffs and sporadically wooded slopes. The peak rose to my left with the narrow ridge we had climbed this morning clearly visible. From the summit the cliffs fell 1,700 metres to the lake, which was now dominated by Gunung Baru, perfectly proportioned with its solidified lava flows stretching out into the water. The sun was directly behind me and the steep rim threw a long shadow that filled half of the huge caldera and crept slowly up Baru's slopes. Clouds moved in below me to the left and travelled gently across the lake. I attempted to capture the scene on film but my 50mm lens wasn't wide enough to do it justice. I zoomed in on the ridge leading up to the peak in order to capture our success only twelve hours earlier.

As the sun fell, the shadows filled the crater and the temperature sharply dropped. Clouds packed the land below me to the west and I felt that the sunset was going to be more of a quick disappearing act. I decided, therefore, to begin my trek to the campsite while there was still plenty of light and with one last reflective look I jogged down the slope. As I got within sight of camp, I could see tents spread out along the grassy ridge, which seemed to be floating in a sea of clouds. At the end of the ridge was a small congregation of bodies quietly facing westwards. I took a photo of the scene as the sun self-effacingly disappeared and five minutes later was greeted by a cheery call of "Hey rosbif".

My tent and Julian and Billa's tent were nestled in a small depression with Rana and Sirip already preparing food. *Les Français* were spread along the ridge ahead of me. Rana, who had uncannily anticipated the exact timing of my return, had made some drinking chocolate kindly donated by Sirip and I gratefully took this and wandered down to chat with Manu. It quickly began to get dark and cold so I wandered back to my tent to put some layers on; by now even the short steps down to my tent hurt. As I sorted myself out the porters were erecting a large awning about four metres in length and spreading it between the back of my tent and Julian and Billa's tent; they were obviously all going to congregate here tonight.

I accompanied Julian by the fire and gradually everyone else joined us. It was to be a communal meal and Didier asked us if we would like to share his group's mushroom soup; this sounded most agreeable so I made myself comfortable and prepared to be waited on. Julian had the bright idea of bringing out roll-mats so I returned to my tent to grab mine and also my cap, scarf and harmonica just in case the festivities called for it.

We were all now sat around the fire waiting to be fed, watching sparks rising optimistically into a night sky embellished by the occasional shooting star. I lay flat on the ground, my feet by the fire trying to keep warm as various cheery comments were thrown around. The food arrived, once again egg-fried rice with a boiled egg – it was nice, and appreciated, but doing my head in. I managed very little and flicked varying amounts into the darkness in an attempt to deplete my plate without offending anyone. The mushroom soup arrived a little later and for a man who doesn't like mushroom soup, I destroyed it with zeal. Cups of tea were circulated, accompanied by friendly banter, and once again the adage "food is incidental to a good meal" was proven.

The request eventually came for music and so I produced my harmonica and played the only tune I vaguely know that's worth playing. It would be interesting to know the highest altitude at which The Beatles' 'Love Me Do' has been played but we pulled it off reasonably well. There are, however, limits to the number of songs you can sing with harmonica accompaniment and so we quickly, almost immediately, in fact, resorted to *a cappella*.

The set list was an eclectic mix of songs old and new but two that particularly stood out were the rosbifs' versions of 'God Save the Queen' (the national anthem, not the Sex Pistols) and 'You'll Never Go To Heaven' ('playtex bra' remix with special limited edition including 'frenchman's car'). I'm sure some Christmas carols crept in there as well.

The comedy section soon followed with Julian and I able to dominate due to English being the lingua franca (a curious paradox). Julian definitely took top billing with a selection of gags ranging from cheesy to disgusting. Easily the most popular, due to its apparent international nature, was:

Why don't Frenchmen have two eggs in the morning?
...because one egg is *un oeuf*.

The French guys thought this was fantastic but Billa, who had initially answered the question with "Don't they?" remained perplexed until the finer points were explained to her. We discussed whether the joke would work in German but concurred very quickly that it wouldn't. Rana came over and asked to borrow a pen, which I duly got for him, and he disappeared with it to play cards with the rest of the porters. After an hour of gags, idle banter and general cheekiness, the exertions of the day began to tell, particularly on me as I lost myself gazing idly upwards at the gently glittering sky. It was time for bed. A squabble broke out about who would find the next lot of wood for the fire so I made my apologies and ambled to my tent. I left the vast expanse of the universe outside and went to sleep.

The Finishing Line
(finding cool waters)

People don't take trips, trips take people

The next thing I knew it was daylight and I could hear chattering outside. I lay there for a while contemplating the walk ahead until someone inquired if I was awake yet. I grunted. It had gone 7:00 but was still cold so I felt extremely averse to crawling from my sleeping bag.

"Neek."

"Neek."

"Yeah?"

"Food."

"Oh. Okay. Just a minute."

I tentatively poked my head out of the tent. It was Rana ready with breakfast – deep-fried bananas in batter – fantastic. I grabbed them with a cup of coffee and skulked back into my cave caring only about food, shelter and warmth – so much for evolution.

Feeling more human and less like a missing link, I resurfaced in an attempt to be sociable; everybody looked equally tired and seemed to want to get this final leg of the journey over and done with. We were told it could take around six hours and instead of appreciating the final hours of a fantastic expedition, I began to mull over the timings of getting down, getting sorted, getting transport from the village and getting to either Sengiggi or Gili Air. I also wanted to see the waterfalls near the village but time was going to be tight. I wandered over to the French camp where we exchanged pleasantries. Didier was once again sorting out his injuries, this time being tended to my Marina. It was too early to be watching *ER* so I returned to our site and the busy cleaning-up session that was going on.

Departure time was approaching so I returned to my tent to prepare myself for the final descent. My feet had begun to hurt on the trek into the caldera yesterday and though there were no obvious signs of damage, I knew that particular pressure points would start hurting. I wrapped various points in the plasters I was so glad I'd brought and carefully put on my filthy socks and boots. I stepped out of the tent and coated the top of my knees, calves, forearms, and face and neck in sun cream and threw some over to Julian and Billa to do the same. Rana sorted the tent and we were ready to go.

The French team were still mooching around so Julian, Billa, and I decided to make a head start – more opportunities for rest on the way, I thought.

We cheerfully began to wander down the dusty track that led through knee-length grass, sparsely populated by trees of varying shapes and sizes. We took a leisurely pace as the path began to steepen and reveal shallow ravines to either side of us. The three of us were the only people in sight as we followed the clear trail over a ridge that revealed an ever-steepening narrow track. After twenty to thirty minutes, I turned to see the French party making their way down the steep path we had just negotiated. The tall trees looked stark against the grass and skyline. Julian took a picture of me with the other group in the distance and we then continued through grass which was now almost up to our shoulders.

We took regular two-minute breaks and after a while the French team had caught up with us. The terrain had now changed from grassy wooded slopes to dense forest and the route was mostly a steep, dusty track with rocks and tree roots for support. Occasionally the path would level out but mostly our feet were either slipping or thudding ever downwards.

From time to time Julian or Didier was behind me but mostly I was happiest at the back, dictating my own pace and deciding on the route of least pain. My legs were hurting but mostly it was the pressure on my feet, particularly the outside of my right foot which I realised I was landing on slightly more heavily. Every footstep was painful and each time I had to step down a slightly higher drop I would wince in anticipation of the hurt. It wasn't anything that made me feel I couldn't make it but it was certainly something that made me want to get this leg of the journey over and done with. The odd thing was that I was still enjoying it.

We stopped by a log for ten minutes for biscuits and water and I took the opportunity to self-consciously renew my plasters on my right foot.

Our trek through the forest continued, the track winding downwards, sometimes down dusty culverts and other times negotiating twisted tree roots that would provide us with perfectly positioned steps and then a big drop. I angled my feet as best I could in an attempt to land flat rather then slightly on the outside like I normally do; from time to time I would let gravity pull me into a run which would give me welcome relief until I had to jolt to a stop to avoid a domino effect on the rest of the group.

As we descended in altitude, the jungle thickened but the well-worn track was very clear. Two or three times we passed trekkers coming the other way whom we encouraged with friendly comments but most of the time we were on our own. Whenever the group was quiet for a bit too long, one of the French guys would spur Julian or I into telling a joke of some description; naturally the quality of these deteriorated with time but the one egg being *un oeuf* joke remained enduringly popular.

I noticed that the porters were beginning to be a bit more noisy. We had been used to them being quietly in the background but they were now chatting away and doing the odd monkey or dog impression. They were clearly full of energy (unlike the rest of us) and I sensed we must be approaching the finishing line. Rana started singing loudly behind me. It was obviously a song with feeling and when he sang the word *merdeka*, which I assumed meant something like 'independence' due to the name of the square in Jakarta, I asked him if it was the national anthem. He said it was and we had a friendly chat about life in Indonesia and the current political situation. He seemed very unimpressed with the current government and was quite scathing on the deposed President Suharto; he felt things were going to change further, hoping for more democracy and a better leader. It was good to take the opportunity to chat to Rana properly and I told him that his impressive grasp of English made me feel embarrassed about my poor Indonesian. He smiled and shared a few Indonesian words and phrases with me, pointing upwards at *mata hari,* literally 'the eye of the day', which was attempting to shine through the trees.

We had been in the jungle for around two hours but abruptly it stopped and we found ourselves by a large sign that looked like some indicator of national park status. We laid down and feasted on biscuits and water – the French guys had some really nice biscuits which they'd been sharing with the group since our stop in the jungle; Julian had some very dodgy pineapple creams.

We had less than an hour to go. The final leg began through reeds four metres high and as the land flattened it became more obviously arable. We spotted goats, then shacks, then finally people. The track widened so we could walk four abreast and our pace quickened as we sensed the end.

Suddenly, with what seemed like little warning, we were there: a collection of wooden houses, and a big sign saying "Coke". We were back at the top end of the village and there was a restaurant right in front of us.

We whooped and yelled the word "Coke" very loudly – quite what it says about 21st century man when he can get so excited about a fizzy, sugary drink, I don't know, but we would have paid huge amounts of money for one of those small bottles.

What a restaurant. They had tables and chairs and everything. All of us wandered around congratulating each other and then wandered around aimlessly for a short while, trying to remember how to conduct oneself in this environment; eventually we did the sitting down thing.

The waiters were frantically opening bottles of coke but as each of us received one we stood there, patiently waiting for everyone to have a drink in their hands. The moment came and with a real feeling of togetherness and pride we toasted each other and our shared experiences; a spirited group of travellers brought together by the same aspiration. Our bottles were emptied in seconds and another round was ordered from the slightly bemused waiters. The French guys took a couple of group photos and we sat there relaxed and reflective. I paid for mine and Rana's cokes and we set off along the track and then down the road to our guest house – all aches and pains now banished.

The guest house was where we'd left it. We ambled into the restaurant area where we had been sitting that early morning that seemed like a month ago and ordered some food. It didn't seem banal to wonder how three days can sometimes seem like hours and sometimes seem like months. I retrieved my backpack from reception and sat down wearily in the shade. It was now time to start thinking about how we were going to get back to civilisation and for me particularly where I was going to go next. The original plan was to go straight to Gili Air, the large island off the west coast, to chill out for a couple of days. I also wanted to visit the waterfalls a few kilometres down the road from here but wasn't sure if I had time as I'd have to get to the main road by about 4:00 to have any chance of getting a bus.

However, another plan was hatching elsewhere. The French posse had booked and paid for transport all the way back to Sengiggi and were planning on a posh hotel and a day trip to Gili Air the next day. They also hoped to visit the waterfalls today on their way down. This sounded like an interesting plan. Whilst all this was going on we exchanged e-mail addresses as it seemed that at least some of us would be disappearing elsewhere. The food came in dribs and drabs and we ate quickly. I chatted about what to do next with Julian and Billa and a plan began to gain momentum. Olivier, Didier and Manu clearly wanted to help us out if they could and with a few minutes bargaining with the guest house owner, another bemo had been booked for the porters and gear and we had our own little van for the seven of us. It was going to be very cosy but so what; this was transport, waterfalls, and a posh hotel in Sengiggi – this was going to be good.

I scribbled some brief notes:

Rinjani = 3,726 metres = 12,000 feet
Sembalan Lawang = 1500 metres = 5,000 feet

1. To plawangan 2 = 2,900 metres = 9,500ft = altitude gain of 1,400 metres or 4,500 feet = 12 kilometres
9 hours instead of 6

2. Plawangan 2 to top = 800 metres or 2,500 feet = 4 hours instead of 3
Top to lake = 1700 metres or 5,500 feet (4 hours from camp)
Lake to plawangan 1 = 600 metres or 2,000 feet = two hours

3. Plawangan 1 to Senaru = 1,800 metres or 6,000 feet = 3 hours
P 1 = 2,634 metres
Lake = 2,000 metres
Baru = 2,351 metres
Lake depth = 230 metres
Rim averages 600 – 800 metres above lake

A bemo turned up for the porters and we bid them fond farewells, pressing 10,000Rp notes into their hands. I thanked Rana for his patience and effort.

"No, you good walker and always smiling. Why you always smiling?" he asked, cheerfully.

"I had very happy time, best time, and you best porter," I said, shaking his hand.

He grinned and made his way to the bemo.

We ensured that all our stuff was carefully packed and then threw it onto the roof of the van where it sat precariously as it was lashed down with rope by the driver. There was, of course, no roof rack and so the ropes went in one side window and out of the other with little adherence to UK traffic legislation or EU health and safety regulations. We took a group photo and I gave my backpack one last lingering, loving look; I assumed that the next time I would see it would be bouncing along behind us leaving a trail of destruction and scattered clothing in its wake.

We crushed ourselves into the van and set off down the steep winding road. It was only five minutes before we stopped and bundled ourselves out opposite a concrete path leading down into a valley. There in the distance amongst the greens and browns of the forest was the narrow white gash of a waterfall descending two or three hundred metres down the cliff face. I hadn't washed for three days. I was looking forward to this.

Long concrete steps led down to the base of the waterfall. The wonderful noise increased in volume and as we turned a corner we could see it in all its perfection, falling in a series of steps, two narrow falls about seventy metres up which then turned into this thirty metre high torrent hitting the water in front of us. The volume of water didn't seem extreme, looking more like a lace curtain than anything else, with a diameter of around four metres and creating a shallow pool which was barely calf-deep. Perfect.

We quickly stripped off our grubby footwear and shirts and negotiated the pebbles in order to be gently caressed by the spray. The fall itself, however, was slightly different; despite its relatively benign appearance, it was still a huge amount of water falling from thirty metres up. It was fantastic to be standing next to it, gradually trying to edge into the water until the force became too great. The mad ones amongst us ran underneath but my burnt shoulders seemed very much against this idea. We shouted and laughed and demanded that photos were taken by Didier who was watching us with great amusement. There is something very special about moments like these and we posed victoriously for more photos. I wished I could be here forever.

Winding Down
(Lombok to Bali to Java to home)

Selamat tinggal

It was time to move on so we trudged back up the steps and squeezed ourselves into the van. Our next stop was to be Bangsal where we were to meet Olivier's girlfriend. It transpired that she and Olivier both worked in Indonesia for a French engineering company – this finally explained Olivier's command of the language. She wasn't there when we arrived so we had a bite to eat whilst we waited and endured constant interruptions from locals asking us if we were going to the Gilis – this was where the boats departed. Eventually she was spotted and we were on the final leg to Sengiggi.

We were making pretty good time until we reached the outskirts of Sengiggi where the road was suddenly blocked by a throng of people and vehicles – all coming in the opposite direction. It was an Indonesian wedding. The van stopped as the hundreds of people filling the streets began to engulf us. Standing on the van we took photos of the slow-moving crowd, girls in huddles, guys in groups and mothers with children. Between them were cars and vans blasting out music, many with large sets of loudspeakers on their roofs. The centrepiece was a number of young girls dressed in long white dresses and their hair tied back and decorated with ornate golden headbands, I assumed the best-dressed one to be the bride but maybe they all were.

The carnival passed and it was late afternoon as we entered the town; Olivier and his girlfriend set about finding us somewhere nice to stay. After stopping at a couple of hotels we ended up at an opulent four-star place towards the edge of town where we negotiated a ridiculously cheap price for the rooms. I shared with Julian and Didier and we paid £4 each by getting a twin room and having the hotel add an extra bed.

The group went for a team swim in the pool and Julian taught me how to dive; it bemused me that I had to fly halfway round the world in order to finally learn how to jump into some water head first. Arrangements for the evening were posh dinner at posh restaurant. We made ourselves as smart as we could and went to the Sengiggi Beach Hotel where apparently they had an excellent Italian restaurant. A big table was awaiting us and we quickly ordered celebratory cocktails. Spirits on an empty stomach – brilliant. This was followed by a no-expense-spared meal that included some particularly excellent pizza. The meal was leisurely, happy and generously financed by Olivier who made the point that he was working in Indonesia whilst getting paid in Euros, the exchange rate was crazy and it would be his pleasure. We returned to our hotel, had another swim and fell into bed.

We were all up for breakfast reasonably early the next day. Julian, Billa and Marina were, I think, going south, and the French were going to the Gilis – they asked me to join them but I made an excuse of having to do laundry and e-mailing so I declined; I actually just felt shagged.

We said our farewells to Julian and Billa; Julian promised to send me some photos, and they were gone. The French team went shortly afterwards leaving me on my own and still taking it all in. I had a relaxing morning watching MTV and having a shave.

It was approaching lunchtime and I took my weary legs for a walk into Sengiggi to do some e-mailing. I found out that Mike was going to be in Kuta over the next couple of days so arranged to meet him. It was a hot day but the breeze coming of the sea felt good and I wandered along the beach looking for a bite to eat. Everywhere was very quiet so I stopped at the first restaurant I came to and ordered a bottle of Coke and some chicken satay. My meal arrived quickly but I had trouble finishing the bitter-tasting meat and returned to the hotel to await the French. They arrived just after sunset after what had apparently been a very choppy boat trip back. The plan for tonight was to go back to our local with some Westerners that Olivier knew.

Back in the same seat on the same table ordering more cocktails I felt drained as if the tiredness was catching up with me; I was relieved when the evening was over. It was only at around two in the morning when I started throwing up that I realised it wasn't the trip or the alcohol that had made me feel rough but something a bit nastier. The satay at lunchtime had tasted off but I'd eaten half of it anyway. Thankfully I had some excellent stomach tablets and after a few hours of unpleasantness they managed to sort me out. How come I lasted three days in the wild and then get food poisoning back in civilisation?

I was up early the next morning and ate as much of the free buffet breakfast as possible. The French team had been desperately trying to sort out a trip to the distant island of Flores and were betting on getting to the airport and using vast quantities of rupiah to bribe themselves on to a plane that was apparently full. I found out later that there's no such thing as a full plane in Indonesia and bribery works.

They left just before me and we shook hands and embraced with the fondness of old friends. We had met by chance and I was very sorry to see them go.

My ferry wasn't leaving until the early afternoon so I leisurely packed my bag and left the hotel. I quickly e-mailed Mike to tell him I should be in Kuta by this evening and attempted to get a lift to the ferry terminal at Lembar. I had been told to avoid the main town of Mataram as there were reports of mass demonstrations and possibly trouble. I had been lucky so far; political crises had passed me by. I wondered about the reality of living in this kind of situation, whether it ate into your being or whether it was something that just happened to other people. I guessed a lot of that depended on whether you were a minority community and, for the people I'd met, how the state of the economy affected your daily life. I hoped the Ranas of the world could continue to make a decent living.

I stood by the roadside and attempted to negotiate with a number of bemo drivers. Getting nowhere, I was approached by a smiling teenager on a small motorbike who offered me a similar price to the bemo guys. The motorbike, whilst being perfectly adequate for a smiling teenager, didn't look suitable for a smiling teenager, scruffy Westerner and large backpack. However, I thought it would be amusing to take him up on his offer. I tightened my backpack to my shoulders, got on behind him and we sped out of town.

We stopped briefly at his house, surprisingly to get helmets, and then joined the main road south. Initially the trip was fine but as we continued I felt my backpack getting heavier and heavier and I wondered at the wisdom of wearing shorts due to the risk of falling off and the burning midday sun. I'd just climbed a volcano and did not want to die on a bloody motorbike. We sped along the hot roads, the backpack eating into my shoulders, the sun eating into my skin, and after what seemed like days we arrived at the terminal.

The ferry journey passed with recollections of treacherous

climbs and happy celebrations; but also the emptiness of being alone after three such intense days.

Five hours passed and I was coming back into Padangbai and trying to come up with a plan to get to Kuta. I decided to see what offers of transport I got at the terminal and if they were no good I would walk to the main road where I had left Diana and Vit and try to hitch a ride. After several offers of around 100,000Rp I decided to take the second alternative and started my walk. As the sun went down I left the town behind me. Darkness set in and fewer and fewer vehicles passed. I was sure that I should have made it to the main road by now and as it steepened I began to consider the intelligence of this plan; I looked up and down the dark, empty road, grinned optimistically and carried on. I had been walking for forty minutes, there was nothing but trees around me, my bag was now feeling very heavy and I was wondering if this was the best decision I had ever made; suddenly there were lights and a friendly beep as a mini-van full of travellers pulled over. The driver asked me where I was going and I told him. I couldn't believe it when he offered me a price of 20,000Rp – I would have happily paid 100,000Rp now, so on I hopped.

Our trip to Kuta was uneventful until on a busy roundabout we stalled and the driver was completely unable to get the van started. Two Germans and I leapt out and heroically volunteered to help by pushing it in an attempt to get it jump started – our immediate success brought great cheers from everyone on board and we continued on. I was dropped by the beach with no clue where I was but luckily had ended up near an area called Poppies Gang 2, which was pretty much where I wanted to stay. I wandered through the dark lanes and found a dodgy-looking block of rooms down a side street. It was cheap and nasty, but I was tired. I agreed to stay. I went for a wander to try and find Mike and ended up at a bar called the Sari Club which opened out onto Jalan Legian and seemed to be the only one with any life, well it was full of Aussie surfers; I assumed if Mike was anywhere this would be a good place to look. No luck so I sauntered back onto the street, avoiding the prostitutes hanging around outside, and ventured back to my humble abode past the two girls offering me oral sex for a £1 ("Hey meester, licky-licky").

In the daylight, Poppies Gang 2, a narrow lane joining the busy Jalan Legian and the beach was filled with stalls, bars and restaurants. I wandered down to the beach which was flanked by a road and a row of palm trees stretching as far as I could see. The beach itself was broad, white, clean and quiet; the sea not quite rough enough for decent surfing. I'd lost the address of where Mike was staying but I vaguely remembered the name and I knew it had a swimming pool. I arrived at a likely looking spot and paid 100Rp for a towel and seat by the pool – here I spent the rest of the day – no Mike. I had planned to leave the next day in order to get a bus to Jogya but some tentative investigations into flights revealed that I could fly in two hours for just £15 rather than suffering an overnight bus – I decided to treat myself. That night I returned to the club and as I walked in I spotted a cream baseball cap I thought I recognised. Jon looked up and his face turned into a grin.

"All right, mate. Small world," he chuckled.

We laughed and caught up on our journeys so far. Jon had flown straight to Kuta from Jakarta and by his own admission was pretty much just hanging out. I asked him what his best bit had been and he leant forward seriously.

"Mate, stay away from the prossies."

I raised my eyebrows and asked him what he meant.

"Well there's these two girls round the corner offering services behind a market stall."

And he proceeded to tell me how he had been lured into their lair for some 'licky-licky' and whilst they were 'distracting' him lost 100,000Rp out of his back pocket.

"Outrageous," he said. "Outrageous. And I paid them fifty thousand."

I laughed saying I would heed his warnings and was secretly pleased that my adventures were slightly less 'adventurous'. We were joined by a few Aussie mates of his and chatted for an hour or so. I wanted to check my e-mails before the nearby place closed so left them to it. No news from Mike so I turned in.

The next day was more time by the pool and a major shopping spree that involved shorts, T-shirts, watches and sundry presents – I amused myself late into the evening developing an rapport with the local traders.

"What your name? What your name?"

"Nick," I replied.

"Like this," one of them said, pointing at some fake Nike shorts.

"Yes, like that," I laughed. And so I had almost-personalised clothing for the rest of the trip.

I sorted out my plane tickets and lift to the airport and decided to have one last look round the Sari Club. Once again no luck so I decided to get an early night.

Making my way out I noticed someone who looked just like Marina, which wouldn't have been so weird had she not been standing next to someone who looked exactly like Billa. It was. I rushed over to them with a yell and after their initial shock we hugged and caught up with their story so far. They had ended up in Ubud, had left Julian there and were here for a little 'civilisation'. It was great to see some of my travelling companions again and we spent the evening drinking cocktails out of litre bottles and dancing. At around 3:00, we once more said our farewells. I negotiated the prostitutes and made a quick phone call home. Then to bed.

I awoke five minutes before my lift to the airport, frantically rushed to be ready and ran to the waiting taxi-van. I was loading my bag into the back when I heard a pretty good Sean Connery impression.

"Mishter Nick, I preshume."

I turned as Mike slapped me on the shoulder and grabbed my hand with a big grin.

"Where the hell have you been?" I laughed.

He pointed down the road and pointed to a hotel I must have walked by several times over the last couple of days.

"Stuck by the pool," he said. "I thought I gave you the address."

"Lost it," I said, grinning. We caught up as best we could for the next couple of minutes but I had a plane to catch so we vowed to catch up on e-mail and I left for the airport. The flight was perfect, including a stunning view of a volcano throwing ash into the air; I guessed it was Semeru saluting or Merapi laughing.

Before lunch I was in Jogya. The taxi dropped me at Jalan Sosro and Ecu was there, waving. I asked him if the little motorbike Ecu, my taxi from Merapi, had been around and he said no so I went and checked myself in to the guest house. I decided to have one of the penthouse suites on the roof – a good idea, I thought, until the next morning when I got the full force of the cockerel and the muezzin. Ecu then took me round to the guitar man and I checked out his handiwork. It looked pretty good except the frets were a bit high so I asked him to sort it out and said I'd pick it up tomorrow.

I walked to the train station in order to sort out my tickets to Jakarta; the booking office held no fear for me this time and I bought them in Indonesian. Having once again checked for Ecu the motorbike, I went for a wander around the town.

Jalan Malioboro was full of troops. Over the road the grounds of a large building were full of people; it seemed to be a major political demonstration and the army were out in force. Dressed in red and black camouflage combats (in case they ever go to war in a poppy field at night, I guess) and red berets, it was possible to identify the important ones by their large dark sunglasses.

Banners were all over the place proclaiming "*REFORMASI –
YES. KEKERASAN – NO*", which I translated as "*Reform – Yes.
Fifty more years of autocratic government – No*", but for all I knew it could
have meant "*Reform – Yes. Bad hair days – No*".

Interestingly, one particularly large banner was next to a
Kentucky Fried Chicken so potentially the message was
"*Reform – Yes. Homogenised global culture – No*" or perhaps "*Reform –
Yes. Reconstituted chicken nuggets – No*".

The situation didn't seem overly tense so I crossed the
road and made my way towards the main gathering. Three
individuals were on a stage addressing a crowd of several
hundred and above them was a banner that appeared to be
demanding some kind of referendum. I tentatively took some
photos of the crowds and assembled armed forces, briefly
considering the risk of getting arrested for that kind of thing
and what the inside of an Indonesian prison might be like.

The people around me appeared unconcerned by my
presence and seemed to be split into groups of those who were
genuinely interested in what was being said and those who were
just hanging out. The guy who enthusiastically asked me to
take a picture of his kid and his mate seemed to be in the
latter group.

The rest of the day was taken up with weaving around curiously
friendly soldiers whilst trying to do some shopping; perhaps this was
a further example of Yogyakarta's enlightened views on political
change. The evening passed by.

The next morning I picked up my guitar and spent the day
wandering and wondering. Perhaps I could have spent that extra
time at Bromo; but then I wouldn't have climbed Rinjani with the
people I did... I wonder what happened to the parallel me in my
parallel universes? I felt bad for the parallel me who fell off the
motorbike; and as for the one who fell into the crater...

Having bidden farewell and thanked everyone I went to the station for my long trip to Jakarta, which was dull and uneventful. I arrived at Gambir station and trudged wearily to Jalan Jaksa.

I found a clean little place to stay and having dumped my stuff decided to go to a major mall and find out about contact lenses as I'd heard they were extremely cheap. I caught a bus that seemed to be going in vaguely the right direction and saw the shiny mall as we shot past it. I got off at the next stop and walked back. On finding an opticians I asked about contact lenses and was offered the opportunity to try a pair for free. I had never worn contacts before and it took me fifteen minutes to get the first one in, aided by a very helpful assistant telling me not to close my eye as I tried to fit it. It was unnatural – she was asking me to touch my eyeball for God's sake. Her offer to do it for me was forcibly refused. Eventually fitted, I wandered around in a state of shock at my ability to see things; even more frighteningly it was the first time I had seen myself properly in twelve years – I wasn't sure if I liked what I saw. I purchased a year's supply for £45. More shopping and then back to the guest house.

I ambled over to the restaurant where I had eaten with Jon on my first day in Jakarta; I wondered what he was up to. A group of Indonesian girls were still giggling in the corner. Sitting at the bar I was approached by a gaunt, wizened man (has the word 'wizened' ever been used outside of children's fantasy books?) who sat down next to me. Half-Chinese, half-Indonesian, I guessed. With the conspiratorial tones of someone offering to sell me nuclear weapons from the back of a lorry he asked me about England and my occupation there. Incongruously this led on to an offer of an export deal:

"I give you good price for wood, batik, everything you want... good money."

Thanking him for his offer and half wondering what would happen if I took him up on it, I took his business card and wandered over to my guest house. Back in my room, I speculated on the implications of forgetting to pay my bill at the restaurant. Back at the restaurant they smiled at me saying that it was okay and that they knew where I lived. I smiled. I bet they did.

It was my final evening and I thought I'd check out the clubs. First stop was my first ever visit to a Hard Rock Café. I was most unimpressed at having to stand in a queue – I was a Western tourist, how dare they make me wait. The entry fee was 20,000Rp including your first drink. I availed myself of a beer and watched the decent covers band on stage. A couple of very pretty local girls, Twiglets in white cotton, came over to chat and ask me who I was. We talked and I soon realised that they were looking for a Western man, living and working here, as a possible partner/husband. In a chivalrous burst of honesty, I told them I was travelling and going home tomorrow. This turned out well as it meant that we could amicably chat and have fun dancing for an hour or so. They told me they were off to another club they liked called JJ's and asked me if I wanted to join them. I told them maybe later and we said farewell. I finished my drink, recognising it could be good fun and so found a taxi and asked him to take me there.

Another 20,000Rp and I sauntered in, spotting them chatting to a few people opposite the bar. They smiled and introduced me to the group – a mix of Westerners and locals. One guy told me that the infamous Tanamur disco, referred to by Jon, was next door and I ought to check out its infamy. I decided I should too and so wandered round the corner and entered the dark and dingy hall. It was packed full of Indonesians, Westerners and prostitutes with pumping dance music coming from every corner. I got a drink and eventually started chatting to a British businessman who was here 'on a job'. A couple of girls befriended us, one of which was about one metre tall and a little overly keen to do 'business'; we all danced for an hour or so and by now it had gone 2:00 so I made an inconspicuous exit and taxied back to the guest house. No money for you, young lady.

Next morning I sorted out a taxi to the airport for 1pm and had a final melancholic wander around the town. Jakarta was ugly but I wanted to embrace it. Walking in contemplation down a quiet alleyway, I had to jump quickly to one side in order to avoid a motorbike being driven by a man and two dozen chickens; there's a metaphor there, somewhere. I spent the rest of the morning on the guest house roof eating mangoes with a penknife and trying to catch some sun. The taxi was prompt and I was on my way. Unfortunately I'd read my check-in time as my flight time so I arrived two hours early.

I cheerily busked with my new guitar; nobody gave me any money.

A day later I was home.

Epilogue

It is probably only in retrospect that you can judge the personality of a journey; whilst you are involved, the intensity clouds your judgement, only when you've parted can you look back rationally and decide whether or not you were well-treated. The average holiday to the Costa del Sol is probably like an over-indulgent uncle, the one who drinks too much at Christmas, embarrasses everyone and goes on about live and let live. The trip to Disneyland is either the guilty parent trying to make up for lost time or the little boy who doesn't want to grow up. Indonesia had a strange personality; I don't know if I'd like to meet it in the street. It would get you into trouble but then get you out again. It would show off and set you challenges that you'd have to do because you'd want to impress it. But ultimately I think it would just about know your limitations and would look after you as best it could. The only problem about hanging around someone like that is that you end up acting like them.

> *'Your travel life has the essence of a dream. It is something outside the normal, yet you are in it. It is peopled with characters you have never seen before and in all probability will never see again.'*

Agatha Christie

I haven't seen my travelling companions since. Mike continued on to Australia, Anna did her doctoring, the French did French stuff, Billa and Julian returned to Japan. A few weeks after my return I received a letter from Tokyo – Julian had sent the photos from Rinjani; I smiled. Soon afterwards there was an e-mail from Manu with a set of photo attachments of happy times on a mountain far away. A couple of months later I received a postcard from Diana and Vit but my attempts to get them by e-mail were in vain; two years passed by and until one day I was amazed to receive an e-mail from Diana (in Germany) saying "Hi" and sorry that she hadn't been in touch. It would be nice to see everyone again.

Indonesia continued to suffer from political and economic problems until Megawati Sukarnoputri, arguably the winner of the elections in 1999, was installed as President in 2001 – depending on who you ask, previous opposition to her was based either on the fact that her party did not have an overall majority or on the fact she was a woman. Many were disappointed that her presidency failed to deliver the significant improvements they had expected and she was defeated by Yudhoyono, the current president, in 2004. On the outer edges of the country there were more extreme problems with violence in East Timor eventually leading to independence in 2002 and continuing civil unrest in the province of Aceh in Sumatra.

However, it is the bewildering number of natural and man-made disasters that have hit Indonesia that have been the most poignant.

On October 12, 2002 in Bali, a suicide bomber detonated a bomb in his backpack inside Paddy's Bar, opposite the Sari Club; fifteen seconds later a Mitsubishi van exploded right outside the Sari Club and the blast tore across the same tables filled with travelling friends that I had laughed and joked at with Marina and Billa. Some of the injuries were horrific and over two hundred people died. In

2005, another series of explosions around Kuta killed a further twenty people.

Bromo surprised many people in 2004 by suddenly erupting and killing two people but this was nothing compared to the earthquake off the coast of Sumatra which on December 26th of that year caused one of the most devastating tsunamis in human history. And then in 2006, following dramatic eruptions from Mount Merapi, a massive earthquake caused the deaths of over 5,000 people in the Yogyakarta area and left over 200,000 homeless; it also caused significant damage to the temples of Prambanan.

Indonesia remains temperamental, unpredictable and demanding; dramatic, intriguing and extraordinary.

And Nick? It was always going to be difficult when there were still parts of me blowing around that steep ridge leading to the summit of Rinjani; or resting on the rim of Batur; or riding around the Sandsea caldera of Bromo. It took another year and another trip to Indonesia but eventually I left my job. It's a Monday morning in September and I'm looking out of the window into my back garden and I'm wondering what I'll be doing in six months time – it's great.

And sitting on the table is a battered 5,000Rp note with the picture of three mysterious crater lakes located on the distant island of Flores, west of Timor and east of Komodo, where the dragons come from. Next to it is a scrappy bit of paper with one word – 'Kelimutu'.

About the author

Nicholas Langston-Able was born and educated in Oxfordshire. He qualified as a teacher in Bristol where he has been living for the last twelve years. His first backpacking trip to south-east Asia was to Singapore, Sarawak (Borneo), peninsular Malaysia and Thailand; he has returned to Thailand twice, leading expeditions with small groups of students.

His travels around Indonesia have included the islands of Java, Bali, Lombok and Sumatra. His last independent trip was to Brunei and Sabah in Borneo where he climbed Mount Kinabalu; his journey then took him to Bali, Flores and Rinca. In 2006 he accompanied a group of students to Sarawak and Sabah as part of a 'World Challenge' expedition.

Nick Langston-Able is also well-known in the Bristol area as an accomplished vocalist and guitarist. He rarely plays harmonica.

To find out more about his journey, visit
www.adventures-in-indonesia.co.uk